CAR BADGES
OF THE WORLD

by T. R. NICHOLSON

Illustrated by A. J. STOKES

American Heritage Press · New York

Phototypeset by BAS Printers Limited, Wallop, Hampshire and
printed in the British Crown Colony of Hong Kong

Library of Congress Catalog Card Number: 71-91800
SBN: 8281−0035-7

ACKNOWLEDGEMENTS

The artist, author and publishers are grateful to the following for their kind assistance in the preparation of this book:

A.C. Cars Ltd.
A.E.C. Ltd.
Mr John M. Algie
Mr G. T. Andrews
The *Autocar*
Automobiles Peugeot
Auto-Union GmbH
Mr Harry Barnes
Bayerische Motorenwerke AG
Mr E. A. Bellamy (Montagu Motor Museum)
Mr C. J. Bendall
Mr N. W. Bertenshaw
Lt. Col. C. H. D. Berthon
Mr Charles L. Betts Jr.
Mr John M. Bland
Mr John Borthwick
Mr R. Burgess
Central Car Service Ltd.
Mr Lindsay Cobb
Mr H. G. Conway
Mr A. C. Cook
Mr R. A. B. Cook
Crossley-Premier Engines Ltd.
Mr W. G. Culley
Mr J. R. Davy
Mr Ian Dussek
Mr Godfrey Eaton
Mr Henry E. Edmunds
Mr J. W. Ellerton
Empresa Nacional de Autocamiones S.A.
Mr D. E. A. Evans
Fattorini & Sons Ltd.
Mr D. C. Field
Mr Douglas Fitzpatrick

General Motors Holden's Pty. Ltd.
Mr G. N. Georgano
Mr David Goode (Armstrong Siddeley Owners' Club)
Mr Derrick Graham
Mr W. B. Hamlin
Mr T. L. Hands
Mr Egon R. Hanus
Mr J. W. Hardcastle
Mr J. M. Hill
Mr Thomas H. Hubbard
Mr G. A. Huddlestone
Mr Peter Hull
Mr Henry Hunt
Mr Inman Hunter
Mr F. W. Hutton-Stott
Japan Motor Industrial Federation Inc.
Mr John Jenkins
Mr Glyn Lancaster Jones
Kaiser Jeep Corporation
Mr H. E. Kingsman
Mr W. Kinsman
Mr Kenneth Krueger
Lancia & Co.
Mr Gordon Lett (Assistant to Rouge Croix Pursuivant of Arms)
Dr Alfred S. Lewerenz
Mr Ivor Linsdell
Lloyd Motoren Werke GmbH
Lord Lyon King-of-Arms
Lotus Cars Ltd.
Mr Philip Mann
Mann & Overton Ltd.
Mr Keith Marvin
Maserati Concession Ltd.

Mr F. Wilson McComb
Mr C. W. Morton
Motokov (Prague)
Motor Imports Co. Ltd.
Mr Hans Otto Neubauer
Nissan Motor Co. Ltd.
NSU Motorenwerke AG
Oldsmobile Division, General
  Motors Corpn.
Mr G. A. Oliver
Adam Opel AG
Mr Desmond Peacock
Mr Jackie Pichon
Mr Michael Pitts
Mr C. Poel, Jr.
Mr Cyril Posthumus
Mr Peter Pringle
Mr Harry Pulfer
Renault Ltd.
Mr Roger Richmond
Mr N. A. Ridley
Mr G. Riemer
Mr Herbert Royston
Russian Cars Concessionaires Ltd.
AB Scania-Vabis
Dr Ing. Friedrich Schildberger

Mr C. W. Scott-Giles Fitzalan
Mr D. Scott-Moncrieff
Mr Michael Sedgwick
Mr Selwyn Sharp (Rolls-Royce
  Ltd.)
Mr Jerrold Sloniger
Steyr-Daimler-Puch AG
Mrs Joan Tapley
Mr David Thirlby
Mr W. R. Tite
Toyo Kogyo Co. Ltd.
Mr B. H. Vanderveen
Van Doorne's Automobielfabrieken
  N.V.
Vauxhall Motors Ltd.
Volkswagen Werke AG
AB Volvo
Mr Hans-Heinrich von Fersen
Mr E. S. White
Mr M. J. D. White
Mr Bruce Whitehouse
Mr Howe B. Willis
Wilmot Breeden Ltd.
Mr Raymond A. Wolff
Mr Jonathan Wood
Mr R. J. Wyatt

CONTENTS

CAR BADGES

HOLDEN *Australia*

Holden & Frost were saddlers and coachbuilders of Adelaide, South Australia from 1886. Motor body building gradually supplanted carriage work from the early 1900s, and an emblem consisting of a winged man holding a car, against a background of a factory, was designed. This was replaced in the 1920s by a new, simpler emblem. The lion of the Wembley Exhibition in London, representing the Empire, was in the news, and a heraldic lion formed the centrepiece of the emblem. Under its paws was a rough-hewn stone, possibly intended to represent the forerunner of the wheel. It is often confused with a globe. The association of General Motors Australia (the 'GM' inside the stone) with Holden goes back to 1923, when Holden's Motor Body Builders became the sole Australian manufacturers of bodies for imported General Motors chassis. The interests of Holden and General Motors were merged in 1931, General Motors Holden being the result. In 1948, the first Holden car appeared. It was designed in America especially for Australian conditions, and is Australia's only home-built car of any significance.

AUSTRO-DAIMLER *Austria*

The most renowned make of car to come out of the Dual Monarchy of Austria-Hungary, symbolized by the double-headed eagle on its emblem, was the Austro-Daimler. In 1899 the premier German motor manufacturer, Daimler, set up a factory at Wiener-Neustadt near Vienna to make its cars. These were known as the Osterreichisches Daimler or Austrian Daimler, which became shortened to Austro-Daimler. Ferdinand Porsche came to the company as designer in 1905, and was famous for the Prince Henry-type Austro-Daimler of 1910. By this time, the influence of the German parent had been thrown off. From now on, the name was best known for expensive high-performance cars of advanced design, made until 1933. The Steyr-Daimler-Puch consortium, makers of the current Steyr-Puch, was founded a year later.

3

STEYR-PUCH *Austria*

The concentric black and white circles forming the Steyr 'half' of the Steyr-Puch emblem represent a shooting target, which is very appropriate. The Osterreichische Waffenfabriksgesellschaft of Steyr went back to 1864, when Josef Werndl set up as a gunsmith. They became famous as the makers of the Mannlicher sporting rifle and other weapons. As well as firearms, motor cycles were made by Steyr Werke A.G., and an experimental motor car followed in 1910. Steyr motor cars were put into production from 1920. The connection with Puch came about indirectly. Johann Puch began to make motor cycles in 1899, progressing to cars seven years later. His factory was in Graz, capital of the province of Styria, which has a white and green coat of arms. The Puch Werke ceased to exist as an independent entity in 1920, when it became one with Austro-Daimler, the most famous Austrian motor manufacturer. The Austro-Daimler-Puchwerke A.G. amalgamated with Steyr in 1934, to form the present Steyr-Daimler-Puch A.G. The name Steyr-Puch is currently applied to Fiats for the Austrian market.

F.N. *Belgium*

The Fabrique Nationale d'Armes de Guerre was Belgium's largest motor manufacturer from the earliest days of this great engineering concern's entry into the field. In the first year of production, 1900, a hundred cars were built. These were cheap, simple economy cars of no originality of design, setting the character of most F.N. models to come. The car's name was formed from the initials of the first two words of the company's name. The latter's guns were its best-known product, and its bicycles had come before its motor cycles and cars. The production of F.N. cars ceased in 1939.

MÉTALLURGIQUE *Belgium*

Belgium's Métallurgique was one of her most spectacular makes, but began modestly enough when the S.A. La Métallurgique, railway locomotive manufacturers, offered a small two-cylinder $4\frac{1}{2}$ h.p. car of German Daimler pattern in 1898. It was the Ernst Lehmann-designed cars of 1905 and later that made the name of the marque, with their combination of speed, advanced design, distinctive good looks, and superb workmanship. The magnificent bodies were all made by Vanden Plas. Métallurgiques were notably popular in England, most being exported across the North Sea. They were also built in Germany as the Bergmann-Métallurgique. Although in 1922 the firm came out with a modern car designed by Paul Bastien, later of Stutz, the overseas markets on which the Belgian motor industry had always depended were now denied to it by tariffs, and the Métallurgique was one of the more distinguished casualties. Its factory and plant were acquired by Minerva and Imperia in 1927. The emblem shown was seen on the flat radiators that preceded the famous vee design of 1907. Most of the latter bore no emblem at all.

MINERVA *Belgium*

The first means of transportation built by the de Jong brothers of Antwerp was the bicycle, but they turned to cars in 1900. These were on French Panhard lines. The company's earliest original design was a great success: the 14 h.p. model of 1905. From then on, they built up their reputation as *La Marque Doyenne* of Belgium with a series of cars, powerful, beautifully made and expensive, which would compare with the world's best. Sylvain de Jong's finest creations were the line of magnificent sleeve-valve sixes and eights of the late 1920s and early 1930s. They died in 1934; victims of the world-wide Depression. There were no new models after 1935, when Minerva absorbed Imperia. Henceforth, the firm's only passenger car was the front-wheel-drive Minerva-Imperia, on Adler lines. The Minerva was named after the Roman goddess (the Greek Athena) who presided over the arts and professions, including crafts and industry. Her head appears on the emblem.

A.C. *Britain*

The initials 'A.C.' derived from Autocarrier. This was the name of a motorized delivery tricycle for tradesmen, with a box body between the two front wheels. It was financed by a well-to-do butcher, John Portwine, and made from 1904 by John Weller, who already made the Weller car in small numbers. A passenger-carrying version arrived in 1907, with a seat in place of the box and the driver and passenger riding tandem, but the first true passenger car to come from the firm was the A.C. Sociable, a side-by-side two-seater three-wheeler of 1909. The letters A.C. were styled to go inside a circle because they were originally seen on the hubcaps. On the Sociable, which had a rear-mounted, air-cooled engine, there was no radiator on which it could appear, but with the coming in 1914 of a new, completely conventional small car with a water-cooled engine and handsome rounded radiator, the badge found its way to the normal position. The surrounding circle had lost its original function, and disappeared after 1925.

ALVIS *Britain*

The name of Alvis, belonging to one of Britain's classic makes of car, was first seen not on an automobile but on a piston. In 1914 G. P. H. de Freville, who had managed the British agency of the French D.F.P. car, set up Aluminium Alloy Pistons Ltd in order to make pistons and castings in this comparatively new material for wartime use. (It may be no coincidence that the D.F.P. pre-war had been one of the first makes of car to use aluminium pistons.) Those that came from de Freville's factory bore the name ALVIS in a triangle rather like the present radiator emblem. The name had no special meaning: it was simply a trademark easy to pronounce in any language. Near the end of the war, de Freville designed a complete car engine. This design, and the Alvis name, were taken over by T. G. John (formerly Works Manager of the Siddeley-Deasy Co., makers of aero engines who had been one of de Freville's customers) and applied to a new car that first saw the light of day in 1920. Thus the Alvis car was born. Early models bore a winged badge with the apex of the triangle uppermost, but most cars have carried the badge illustrated.

ARGYLL *Britain*

Scotland no longer produces its own native breeds of car, but in the past there have been more than fifty, and of these at least three were well known outside their homeland—Arrol-Johnston, Albion and Argyll. Of these the Argyll was the most famous. The name was devised by Alexander Govan, the company's founder. In its palmy days, before the First World War, it was at one time the fifth biggest car manufacturer in Britain. For a spell around 1907, Argyll were making cars faster than any other manufacturer in Europe. A grandiose new factory had been opened at Alexandria near Glasgow in the previous year, its name being recorded on the badge illustrated. The red lion in the centre has on its left the thistle, both features of the Royal Arms of Scotland, and for some reason unrecorded, a rose on the other side. This particular badge was used on certain models only, between 1912 and 1922.

ARMSTRONG SIDDELEY *Britain*

Sir W. G. Armstrong Whitworth & Company made the Wilson-Pilcher motor car, with its earliest application of the Wilson epicyclic gear and pre-selection, in the latter years of that vehicle's existence, then turned to making the Armstrong-Whitworth, a solid and conventional machine which was killed off by the First World War. The contemporary Siddeley-Deasy Motor Car Company was formed in 1911 from the fusion of John Siddeley's Siddeley Autocar Company, recently broken away from Wolseley, with the Deasy Motor Car Manufacturing Company. The resulting Siddeley-Deasy car was another orthodox, well-made beast with nothing special to recommend it. In 1919 the two concerns were merged, and a new car called the Armstrong Siddeley began to be made by Armstrong Siddeley Motors Ltd of Coventry. It was designed initially as a luxury car selling at a non-luxury price, and although still cheaper models were made, it never departed very far from this intention. Heavily and beautifully made on an architectural scale, they toyed briefly with a lighter, more elegant line, just after the Second World War. The emblem of the sphinx, seen in more or less stylized form on most Armstrong Siddeleys, dated back to the earlier days of the car, after a journalist described it as being 'as silent and inscrutable as the Sphinx'. The design was based on drawings taken of the Sphinx on London's Embankment. It incidentally supported the impression of massive solidity conveyed by the Siddeley's ultimate successor.

ASTON MARTIN *Britain*

Before the First World War, Lionel Martin and Robert Bamford were distributors of the Singer car. Martin raced modified versions of the Singer, and also other 'specials'. He gained some successes at the speed hill climbs held on Aston Clinton hill in Buckinghamshire. When he came to manufacture his own car in 1921, he gave it the first part of the hill's name and his own surname. The first Aston Martin badge consisted simply of the monogram 'AM' inside a circle, but from 1927 the more familiar winged emblem was substituted. The first in which the wings were stylized, as in that illustrated, appeared in 1932. It was designed by S. C. H. ('Sammy') Davis, the racing driver and sporting journalist. Originally, the name 'Aston Martin' was hyphenated in this pattern of badge.

AUSTIN *Britain*

After leaving Wolseley, Herbert Austin in 1906 set up in business to make motor cars on his own account, and under his own name. The cars, though very well made, were unoriginal in design; though the same could not be said of the emblem that Austin chose. It was said by the company to represent 'rapid, controlled, wheeled motion'. The wings and the stylized dust at the apex of the triangle signified speed. The road wheel on an axle, seen edge-on, represented motion, while the steering wheel stood for control of the whole impossible-looking assemblage of bits. It was typical of the untidy symbolism commonly used to represent speed around the turn of the century. The original emblem was deeper and narrower than that illustrated, which was introduced on 1931 model Austins.

BEAN *Britain*

A. Harper Sons & Bean, who had made motor-car components, took over
the Perry car in 1919 and began to make passenger cars under the name
of Bean. The first Bean was a Perry, modified to enable it to be made by
American mass-production methods. Indeed, an American engineer from
Willys-Overland helped them to install a moving assembly line, the first
in Britain. The cars were made in the town of Dudley, Worcestershire.
The crest on the town's coat-of-arms, which was also that of the Earl of
Dudley, was a blue lion's head. The lion may also have been chosen to
emphasize the Britishness of the Bean, one of the foremost competitors of
the American makes flooding into Britain around 1920. Its selling
organization was called the British Motor Trading Corporation.

BENTLEY *Britain*

Before the First World War, W. O. Bentley distributed a French car, the
D.F.P., in Britain, and developed a sports version of it. After the war,
during which he designed the successful BR1 and BR2 aero engines, he
joined with F. T. Burgess, who had been responsible for the racing
Humbers of 1914, to make the Bentley. Largely thanks to wins in the
24 Hours Race at Le Mans in 1924, 1927, 1928, 1929 and 1930, the
Bentley became one of the most famous British sports cars ever built.
However, the company was repeatedly beset by financial troubles, and
in 1931 went down for the last time. The name was acquired by Rolls-
Royce, who applied it to a completely new and different concept; a fast
luxury car based on Rolls-Royce components. The emblem illustrated
is from one of the latter cars, first offered for sale in 1933. It differs from
that found on W. O. Bentley's cars in being a less delicate design, with
fewer feathers in the wings and generally less detail work.

BRISTOL *Britain*

The Bristol, a fast luxury car of modern design, was first made in 1947 by the Bristol Aeroplane Company, which took its name from the fact that the works was near the city of that name; at Filton, on its outskirts. The Aeroplane Company was one of the earliest and most famous aircraft manufacturers in Britain, and had been turning out a succession of notable designs since 1910. The current Bristol is made by Bristol Cars Ltd, at the same address, for the Aeroplane Company was divorced from it in 1960. The car's emblem shows the arms of the city of Bristol. Naturally enough, for Bristol was and is a major port, the arms illustrate a ship sailing from a city which is a port. The inscription '2 litre' refers to the cubic capacity of the first model's engine.

CROSSLEY *Britain*

F. W. and W. J. Crossley—Crossley Brothers—of Manchester began to make stationary gas engines in 1866, thus becoming the first British firm to take up the four-stroke internal combustion power unit pioneered by Otto & Langen of Deutz in Germany. Later they made the Daimler engine under licence, and it was J. S. Critchley, formerly of the British Daimler factory, who designed the first Crossley car in 1904. Crossleys gained their reputation as very well-made, solid family cars. They gained fame for their record of reliability in wartime conditions in 1914–18, and subsequently for their patronage by British Royalty. The last Crossley passenger cars were built in 1937. Thenceforth, commercial vehicles absorbed the company's efforts. It was absorbed by A.C.V. in 1951, and five years later the name disappeared entirely. The origins of the cross that was the car's trademark have been lost: it can only be supposed that it was chosen as a pun. Certainly crosses feature largely in the arms of families named Cross, Crosse and Crossley.

17

DAIMLER *Britain*

The financier H. J. Lawson's ambition was to establish a 'corner' in the British motor industry from its very birth. His aim and methods may not have been admirable, but his foresight, his vision of the future of the motor car, was ahead of that of most of his contemporaries. His British Motor Syndicate in 1895 bought the German Daimler patents for Britain, and the English Daimler Motor Company was founded in the following year to exploit them. The new factory at Coventry began to turn them out in 1897, under the name of Coventry-Daimlers. Sales were never remarkably good, but with the collapse of Lawson's empire, a reorganized company began to turn out a line of large, fast, well-built, if conservative chain-driven machines that were well-publicized and popular, taking the famous fluted radiator to most corners of the globe. When Daimler became the first European manufacturer to adopt the American Knight sleeve-valve engine in late 1908, the make became associated firmly with the dowager-duchess market, dominating it at the level that could not afford a Rolls-Royce but wanted something equally distinguished, leaning towards stuffiness in preference to ostentation. Daimler retained this image after the sleeve-valve engine was dropped in the 1930s, and has not entirely lost it even today, when the most formal Daimlers are capable of speeds in excess of two miles a minute, and the name is associated with that of Jaguar. The emblem shown was borne by the SP250 sports model.

FRAZER NASH *Britain*

In 1910, A. Frazer-Nash and H. R. Godfrey joined up to make the G.N. cyclecar (G for Godfrey, N for Nash). The crude cyclecar went out of fashion in the early 1920s, and the G.N. died, but Frazer-Nash developed a stark and fierce sports car from it, retaining the G.N.'s dog clutches, chain drive and a differential-less rear axle. The company continued to make this car until 1938, for its efficiency and fine handling qualities had gained it a devoted following. Although Frazer-Nash the man used a hyphen in his name, his car did not. W. H. Aldington, who controlled the firm from 1931, meanwhile introduced the German B.M.W. into England, offering it as the Frazer Nash-B.M.W. After the Second World War, the Frazer Nash reappeared, still as a sports car of the fiercer sort, but now completely modernized, with a B.M.W.-based Bristol engine, tubular frame and independent suspension. The new generation of Frazer Nashes came to an end in 1963

H.R.G. *Britain*

The H.R.G. of the radiator emblem illustrated here formed initials, but whose is not certain. They were either those of Halford, Robins and Godfrey, the partners behind the car, or those of Godfrey alone: H. R. Godfrey, who until the early 1920s was associated with A. Frazer-Nash in the G.N. cyclecar. Frazer-Nash went on to make the sports car bearing his own name, but Godfrey, though he repaired G.N.s and modified Austin Sevens, did not return to motor manufacture on his own account until 1936. Although it had no direct links with the Frazer-Nash, the two cars had much in common—simplicity, light weight, stiff quarter-elliptic suspension, fine handling qualities, and a sporting performance. However, the H.R.G. used normal shaft drive and a conventional gearbox.

HILLMAN *Britain*

William Hillman had his early experience in bicycles, with Coventry Machinists and with the Hillman & Herbert Cycle Co. in the 1870s. His Auto Machinery Company made power units for bicycles; then in 1907 he joined with Louis Coatalen, the French designer, in the Hillman-Coatalen Motor Car Company to make the Hillman-Coatalen car. This was soon dropped, Coatalen going on to make his name with Sunbeam, and Hillman came to concentrate on small to medium-sized cars for the popular market, the most popular Hillman model being the Minx, first introduced in 1931. The emblem illustrated was fitted to the Hillman Minx of 1934–8. The three spires are symbolic of Coventry, popularly known as 'The City of the Three Spires'. These are of St Michael's Cathedral, Grey Friars' Church and Holy Trinity Church. The first winged emblem appeared on Hillmans around 1928.

HUMBER *Britain*

Thomas Humber's machine was one of the earliest and best British bicycles, dating from 1868, becoming famous as a two-wheeler long before a car first appeared under the name. The company was absorbed in 1896 by the financial promoter H. J. Lawson. It was supposed to build cars for him, but those that appeared were long in coming, few, and mostly bad. Four years later, a re-formed and independent Humber company began to make light cars seriously, and from 1905 the name became associated with solid, well-built touring cars of conventional design. They have remained so ever since. The Rootes brothers gained control in 1928. The name is now under Rootes Group, and ultimately Chrysler, control.

INVICTA *Britain*

In 1925 Noel Macklin, who had been partly responsible for the Eric-Campbell and the Silver Hawk, both sporting light cars of no special distinction, joined with J. G. Parry Thomas, designer of the great Leyland Eight and other advanced motor cars, and now a consultant designer, to make the Invicta. Their idea was to create a car combining the best in British and American design—the quality and craftsmanship of the first, the flexibility of the second. The name is the Latin adjective for 'unconquered'. Until 1929 high performance was not among the Invicta's main selling points, but in that year emerged the $4\frac{1}{2}$-litre model, which brought the make its greatest fame, notably in low-chassis, '100-m.p.h.' form. Smaller models were made as well, until production ceased in 1935. Macklin went on to make the Railton, a car of similar conception. Three years later three new models based on the Delage and Talbot-Lago from France were planned, but never appeared. For a couple of years after the Second World War, a new, luxurious model called the Black Prince, with automatic transmission and independent suspension all round, was made. This was Invicta's last gasp, after which A.F.N. Ltd, who made the Frazer Nash, took over.

INVICTA

JAGUAR *Britain*

William Lyons first displayed his business acumen at the age of twenty, when, in the early 1920s, he helped transform William Walmsley's tiny motor cycle sidecar concern into the Swallow Sidecar Company, which prospered through offering attractive variations on the normal, utilitarian appendage at competitive prices. Lyons carried the same principle into the car field when, from 1927, he began offering Swallow bodies on the Austin Seven, Fiat, Morris, Swift, Wolseley, and Standard popular chassis. The Standard Swallow evolved into the S.S., introduced late in 1931. It was Lyons' first original concept, offering rakish elegance and the appearance of speed in its long, low lines for a notably low price combined with the proven reliability and availability of mass-produced mechanical components. The latter were specially designed by Standard for Lyons. The ensemble proved extremely popular in the drab Depression years. The name Jaguar appeared in 1936, and a year later the Jaguar mascot appeared. Cars from this time until the war were called S.S. Jaguars, the initials being finally dropped with the post-war models. The name 'Jaguar' has no special significance, being adopted at a time when aero engines as well as cars in profusion were being named after birds and beasts of prey. The Lyons formula of low price, high quality and high performance became world famous with the XK120 of 1948 and its successors. The emblem shown belongs to the 2.4-litre sedan, the smallest of the range made alongside the E-Type sports car. Its central feature is the Jaguar's head.

JENSEN *Britain*

The Jensen brothers, F. Alan and Richard A., first became known to the British motoring public by designing attractive bodies for attaching to cheap mass-produced chassis of the late 1920s and 1930s in order to give their owners something different. Commercial bodies were also built. Their passenger-car bodies were made by Avon, the coachbuilders, and were seen on many makes, including Wolseley, Morris, Ford, and especially Standard. William Lyons of Jaguar became famous in the same way, and similarly, again, the Jensens took the logical step of building their own cars. The first Jensen, from the beginning a fast, good-looking, expensive touring car, was offered by Jensen Motors of West Bromwich, Staffordshire, in 1936. The brothers continued to make bodies for other firms after the Second World War, and also offered light commercial vehicles.

JOWETT *Britain*

It is not inappropriate that an engine should feature so prominently in the Jowett emblem, for in its earlier days the firm's power unit was the most famous part of its car. Indeed, Benjamin and William Jowett started by making engines alone, for stationary work and for powering other people's cars. However, in 1910—the date on the emblem—the brothers first offered for sale their famous small car powered by their even more renowned flat-twin engine. This was 'The Little Engine with the Big Pull', of less than a litre's capacity, yet able to pull comfortable bodywork at a reasonable speed because it developed its small power at low engine revolutions. In modified form, it was used as late as 1953 in the Jowett Bradford truck. It is illustrated in elevation in the emblem, the transverse horizontal cylinders being clearly visible.

LAGONDA *Britain*

Wilbur Gunn's intended career was that of opera singer, but unlike Campari, the Italian racing driver who later abandoned cars for arias, Gunn dropped his chosen *métier* in 1904 in favour of making tricars at Staines in Middlesex. He was an American, who named his cars after Lagonda Creek, Ohio, which had been his home. His first four-wheeled cars appeared in 1907, but they did not become famous until the advent of the Two Litre model in the late 1920s. Thereafter, with some exceptions, they tended to become bigger and more luxurious. In 1947 Lagonda ceased its independent existence and became part of the David Brown empire, with Aston Martin.

LANCHESTER *Britain*

Of the three Lanchester brothers, Frederick William was the most talented and original. His first car of 1895 was designed from scratch as a motor-car, owing nothing to the horse-drawn carriage, and was unique at the time in bearing no signs of stationary-engine design or power transmission. By 1904, the Lanchester car had pioneered, among other features, disc brakes, the torsional vibration damper for crankshafts, splined drive shafts, the accelerator, pre-selector control of epicyclic gears, worm final drive, aluminium bodywork, and the modern ideal combination of rigid frame with soft suspension. Nor was this the end of Lanchester's ingenuity: he was a student of aeronautics whose contribution to the science was of fundamental importance. George Lanchester was responsible for the design of the cars made between 1912 and 1931, after which he went to Alvis to design motor cars and military vehicles. Frank was the administrator and salesman of the trio. In 1931, the B.S.A. group of companies took control, and the Lanchester name was applied to what gradually became a line of cheap Daimlers. The badge illustrated is from one of these later Lanchesters. Earlier cars had either carried no radiator emblem, or else borne a rectangular badge on the honeycomb. Now that the name was applied to the radiator shell, an emblem shaped to follow the line of the top of the radiator was introduced.

LEA-FRANCIS *Britain*

The design of the Lea-Francis emblem is attributed to R. H. Lea, whose firm of Lea & Francis Ltd of Coventry, Warwickshire, made bicycles before building its first cars in 1904. In the same year production was stopped and Singer took over the design. Car manufacture was not resumed until 1920; in the interim, motor-cycles were made. R. H. Lea is said to have found inspiration for his emblem while on the extensive foreign travels he undertook for his company before the First World War. The heraldic beast in the centre, its fore hoofs on the monogram 'LF', is a sea-unicorn, a rare and apparently late arrival in heraldic zoology which may have originated in Germany. Very little is known about it. The cars bearing the device continued to be made in fits and starts— from 1920 to 1934, from 1938 to 1953, and (fleetingly) in 1960.

LOTUS *Britain*

The Lotus sports and racing cars grew out of a 'special' built for trials by Colin Chapman. From 1952 it appeared as an Austin-engined racing car, and began to be offered for sale in kit form with Ford and other engines. The Lotus was also sold complete. Thereafter it progressed to the most sophisticated modern sports and racing-car designs, though still offering kit cars as well. The derivation of the name Lotus has not been revealed, and the three-sided lozenge that surrounds it and the monogram may have been chosen simply as a convenient shape. The monogram is of Colin Chapman's initials—A.C.B.C., for Anthony Colin Bruce Chapman.

M.G. *Britain*

In 1922, Cecil Kimber became general manager of the Morris Garages, the Oxford retail outlet of William Morris's growing factory at Cowley, just outside the town. Two years later, in answer to an established demand for mildly-tuned, better-handling, better-looking variants of standard touring cars, he began to produce modified Morris Oxfords under the name of the M.G. Super Sports, the initials being those of his firm. With the coming of the first M.G. Midget in 1928, itself based on the Morris Minor, the success of M.G. was assured, for this was the first truly cheap and practical sports car for the masses to emanate from a British factory. Kimber is said to have devised the famous octagon motif, the significance of which, if any, is not recorded.

MORGAN *Britain*

The 1920s and 1930s were the heyday of the three-wheeler in Britain, when a tax dispensation gave them an advantage over four-wheelers, and before customers buying their way into car ownership at the lowest end of the scale became more sophisticated, and more prosperous. H. F. S. Morgan made his first three-wheeler in 1909, putting it into small-scale production a year later. The 'Moggie', though fairly primitive, had an excellent power-to-weight ratio and good road-holding for a three-wheeler, so was popular with sportsmen as well as minimal motorists. However, tastes changed, and the tricycle died in 1950. By this time it had already acquired most 'proper-car' characteristics, except a wheel at each corner, and long before, in 1936, a four-wheeled Morgan had appeared beside it. This was the 4/4, of which the radiator emblem is shown here. In Series 2 form, it is still current at the time of writing; a life of thirty years.

MORRIS *Britain*

William Richard Morris began repairing, dealing in and making bicycles and motor cycles in Oxford while still in his teens. The first Morris motor cycle was shown in 1903. He went into the motor trade, and in 1910 decided to build a motor car of his own. The result, in 1912, was the Morris Oxford, so called after the city of its birth. In fact the new works where it was built was in Cowley, just outside Oxford, and this suburb gave its name to the new model Morris of 1919. William Morris concentrated upon an economy car, as having the best potential market, and at first assembled it—albeit extremely well—from other manufacturers' proprietary parts, including an engine of American Continental origin. Morris's expansion began when he started to make his own parts and acquire his sources of supply, enabling him to increase production and cut prices. He next diversified his range of cars, taking over Wolseley in 1926. M.G. (Morris Garages) had already begun, as a direct offshoot of Morris, and in 1938 Lord Nuffield (as he had by then become) took under his wing the Riley company. Morris Motors became part of the British Motor Corporation in 1952. The Morris emblem shown features part of the arms of the city of Oxford: the ox crossing the ford.

NAPIER *Britain*

D. Napier & Son of Lambeth in London had been founded in 1808, and developed in the nineteenth century as makers of precision engineering machinery such as printing presses and weighing apparatus. In 1898 Montague Napier modified a racing Panhard for S. F. Edge, the sportsman, giving it a more efficient engine and wheel steering. This was the beginning: in 1900, Napier, with Edge in charge of the selling side, began to build cars under his own name. Thanks principally to Edge, the Napier became the most famous British car on the road until the arrival of the Rolls-Royce Silver Ghost. It won the 1902 Gordon Bennett race, but was best known as a well-built, expensive luxury car of ample proportions, which popularized the six-cylinder engine in Britain. Its slogan was 'The Proved Best Car'. No Napiers were built after 1924.

RILEY *Britain*

William Riley was a master weaver who in 1890 took part in the bicycling boom by buying Bonnick & Company, cycle makers. The Riley Cycle Company was formed in 1896, and within three years an even newer form of transportation was explored when a motor tricycle and quadricycle were made. Motor bicycles followed. Percy Riley and the Riley Engine Company, founded in 1903, made power units for Rileys and other makes. The first Riley four-wheeled motor cars came in 1906, and the most famous Riley ever built was certainly the Nine, designed by Hugh Rose, current for around ten years from 1927. In its fundamentals, the design, much modified, formed the basis for the E.R.A. racing car of the 1930s. The last cars of the new line that had begun in 1927 did not vanish until the 1950s, with the end of the Riley 1½- and 2½-litre models.

ROLLS-ROYCE *Britain*

A Manchester manufacturer of electric cranes, F. H. Royce, assembled a car in 1903 for his private use. Royce put it together so carefully that although the engine had only two cylinders, it was remarkably quiet and smooth. Two others were built, and in 1904 Royce went into manufacture. The Hon. C. S. Rolls, a well-known motorist and motor trader, was to look after the selling side. The car was renamed Rolls-Royce. The company, named Rolls-Royce Ltd, also made three-, four- and eight-cylinder cars, but in 1906 the famous six-cylinder Silver Ghost arrived, and from 1907 until 1925 no other model was offered. The design of badge shown here was introduced on the Silver Ghost. The lettering was red until 1930, when a change was made to black. Most Rolls-Royces sold were black, and around this time, stainless steel and chromium plate finishes were introduced for the brightwork. The engine finish was black with aluminium castings, so the overall effect was black and white, matt or bright. The radiator emblem was changed to fit in with the general effect, not in order to mark the death of Royce, as is generally thought. The latter lived until 1933.

ROVER *Britain*

Like so many other makes the world over, the Rover began life as a bicycle; in this case a very famous one. The 'safety bicycle' which is the pattern of the modern machine was first made in large quantities in the 1890s by John Kemp Starley of Coventry, under the name of Rover. It was Starley, too, who had patented the differential gear in 1877 when he had first started to make bicycles. Motor bicycles followed in 1903 and a single-cylinder car a year later. Rover light cars were the best known of the company's products during the 1920s, but since then its image has been one of high-quality, medium-priced luxury. The emblem, suitably enough, is a head-on view of a Viking ship under sail, with a Viking's head clad in the traditional, if inaccurate, winged helmet as a figurehead.

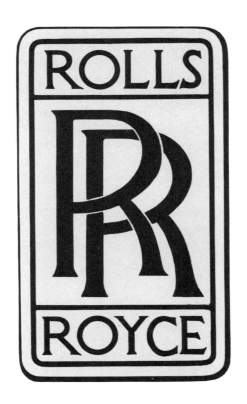

SINGER *Britain*

George Singer of Coventry began making bicycles as early as 1876, and it was for two-wheelers that his name was first famous. There was no connection with the Singer sewing machine. The Singer Cycle Company went on in 1901 to make motor bicycles, in which the engine was contained inside the rear wheel. Motor tricycles were made too, with the engine in the front wheel. Later, a more orthodox design was substituted. In 1903 the Singer Motor Company was formed to build motor cars, taking over the first Lea-Francis design. In later years the company was best known for its highly successful economy cars, starting with the Ten of 1912. The Singer Junior of the late 1920s and its ultimate derivatives, including the Le Mans model sports car of the 1930s, were the most famous cars to bear the name, which was ultimately swallowed up in the Rootes Group.

STANDARD *Britain*

R. W. Maudslay was a civil engineer who set himself up in the motor industry in Coventry in 1903. Alex Craig, who had been a consulting motor engineer, now worked for Maudslay and designed, at his request, 'a car to be composed purely of those components whose principles have been tried and tested and accepted as reliable standards. In fact', said Maudslay, 'I will name my car the Standard car.' In 1908 the Union Jack was seen for the first time on Standard cars, as a symbol of all-British manufacture. The emblem shown was introduced in 1931. Its wings were intended to suggest speed, freedom and power. The artist had in mind the wings of the mythical griffin, half eagle and half lion. In the 1920s the company introduced a Roman standard as a mascot; a further play on words.

STAR *Britain*

Edward Lisle founded the Star Cycle Company in 1886. A star formed the emblem of his machines. Eleven years later, Edward's son Joseph brought a German Benz car from Holland, and in 1898 the company began to make Star cars on Benz lines. The Star Motor Company was formed in 1899 to build cars, while the original firm continued to produce bicycles. The earliest Star car emblems were seen in 1907, when a plain six-pointed brass star was riveted to the top of the radiator shell. It continued until 1925, when it was replaced by a red and green enamelled emblem bearing the words Star Engineering Co. Ltd, Wolverhampton: the company had been renamed in 1904. Sidney Guy, the commercial vehicle manufacturer, took over in 1929. The last Star cars, solid, high-quality touring machines, were built in 1932. At one time, the Star Engineering Company were able to compel Daimler of Germany to sell their cars in Britain without a star emblem.

SUNBEAM TALBOT *Britain*

Sunbeam Talbot was an amalgam of two of the most famous names in British motoring. The name Sunbeam, which is still on the roads, was originally applied to bicycles, and was first seen on a motor-car in 1901. The Sunbeam became renowned as a solid, conventional, high-quality touring car, and at the other extreme, as a racing car that won the 1923 French Grand Prix, among other events. The Talbot was originally called the Clément-Talbot, being the French Clément car imported into England. Among its financial backers was the Earl of Shrewsbury and Talbot; hence the name. After making cars basically of the same type as Sunbeam, a line of very advanced and efficient machines was introduced by the Swiss designer Georges Roesch in 1926. The Clément-Talbot company was taken over by Darracq in 1919, which firm also absorbed Sunbeam a year later. However, in 1935 the Rootes brothers gained control of the Clément-Talbot end of the Sunbeam Motor Car Co. The cars of the new concern were called Sunbeam Talbot from 1938. The Talbot name was gradually dropped from the models, and finally disappeared in 1955. The emblem shown incorporates the word 'Supreme', associated with Sunbeam, and the badge of the Earl of Shrewsbury and Talbot, always seen on Talbots. The beast is not a lion but a talbot, a breed of large hound formerly used for tracking and hunting, characterized by long hanging ears, powerful jaws and a keen scent.

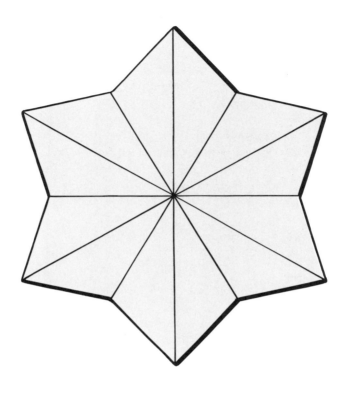

SWIFT *Britain*

Swift of Coventry were typical of a number of firms that later turned to motor cars in that they started life in 1859 as the Coventry Sewing Machine Company, then went on to bicycles ten years later when a Mr Rowley B. Turner showed them a French Michaux bicycle. They made a tricycle for the Prince of Wales in 1882. From there it was a natural and common progression to motor tricycles and quadricycles, and to their first car proper in 1900. The name became best known for solid small cars for the motorist of modest means, and so remained for the rest of its life. The emblem shows swifts as a suggestion of speed, and a shamrock symbolic of the interest of the Irish Du Cros family in the company.

TRIUMPH *Britain*

The Triumph Motor Company of Coventry offered its first car in 1923; a solid modern family sedan of American inspiration. In the late 1920s they tried to invade the mass-produced economy car market with the Triumph Super Seven, but did not have the resources to fight the big battalions of Morris, Austin, Singer and Standard. During the 1930s, the company became best known for fast touring cars of medium size and price, notably the Southern Cross model. It lost its independence in 1945 to the Standard Motor Company. The origins of the emblem are full of mystery. A multi-coloured globe, with British possessions in traditional red, was used on all models until 1937–8. Nowadays, the emblem is in red for the land and blue for the sea.

43

TROJAN *Britain*

The Trojan qualities of strength and steadfastness were supposed to be embodied in the small economy car of that name which emerged from the Kingston-on-Thames works of Leyland Motors Ltd in 1922, accounting for its name and for the Trojan warrior's head that formed the mascot. With its combination of low price, simplicity and ruggedness, it aimed at the mass market dominated by Ford, but failed because of its unconventionality: a two-stroke engine, epicyclic transmission, chain drive, solid tyres and sheer, uncompromising ugliness. The Trojan, designed by Leslie Hounsfield, was also unusual in being built (at first) by a manufacturer of commercial vehicles whose only passenger car to date had been the most expensive luxury machine on the British market. The Trojan was considerably modernized at the end of the 1920s, but after 1934 the passenger car disappeared in favour of commercial vehicles, diesel, gasoline and electric, power units for various uses, go-karts, the Lambretta scooter, and a great diversity of other engineering products. Trojan have taken over the Heinkel bubble-car from Germany, and the Elva sports car.

VAUXHALL *Britain*

Alexander Wilson, a Scottish engineer, founded the Vauxhall Ironworks at Lambeth in London in 1857. It made steam engines for tugs, paddle steamers and other river craft. Experiments with petrol engines for launches came in 1896, and the first motor car was offered for sale seven years later. The name 'Vauxhall' derives from Fulk le Bréant, who was given the manor of Luton for his services to King John. He was also given an heiress for a bride, who brought with her a house at Lambeth, then near London. The house became known as Fulk's hall, whence comes the name. The griffin in the centre of the emblem, a heraldic beast half eagle and half lion, was Fulk le Bréant's device. By coincidence, it was to Luton in Bedfordshire that the company moved in 1905, which accounts for the town's name on the emblem.

WOLSELEY *Britain*

As a young man Herbert Austin worked in Australia for the Wolseley
Sheep Shearing Machine Company. He returned to England to join the
recently-formed British Wolseley concern in 1893. In 1895 he designed
a small car on the lines of the French Bollée three-wheeler. A second
three-wheeler followed in 1896, and a four-wheeled car three years later.
The Wolseley motor car was put into production in 1900. Austin left in
1906 to make cars under his own name; machines that included the
famous Seven. Wolseley continued to make their name for solid family
cars. They came under the wing of William Morris in 1927, and the name
was eventually reunited with that of Austin in the British Motor
Corporation of today.

SKŎDA *Czechoslovakia*

Emil von Skŏda founded the Skŏda Works at Pilsen in 1866 to make
armaments. By 1899, a new group of companies forming the Skŏdovy
Zavody was manufacturing locomotives, engines and general
engineering products as well as arms. By the early 1920s, they were also
making tractors and aircraft engines, and went into car manufacture first
by taking over the RAF (Reichenberger Automobil Fabrik) firm, and
then the famous Bohemian house of Laurin-Klement. From 1925, Skŏda
cars were built. They included, at first, the luxurious Hispano-Suiza
from Spain made under licence, since the company owned the Czech
rights in Hispano-Suiza patents, but from the beginning most Skŏdas
were-mass-produced economy cars. The Skŏda car is now divorced from
its original manufacturers, and is made by the concern responsible for
the Tatra. Its emblem, much stylized, is a winged arrow.

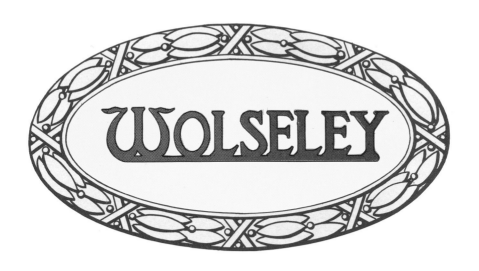

TATRA *Czechoslovakia*

The first gasoline car built in what was then the Austro-Hungarian
Empire was made at Koprivnice (Nesselsdorf) in 1897. It was based on
the successful Benz from Germany. The Koprivnice works was already
known for horse-drawn carriages and railway rolling-stock. Its car was
called the President. Some very advanced designs emanated from the
factory before the First World War; the man responsible, Hans
Ledwinka, offered a car with front-wheel brakes in 1910 and unit
construction of engine and gearbox in 1913. The firm was renamed the
Tatra Motor Works after the war, and in 1921 offered a truly
revolutionary but highly successful machine under the Tatra name, also
designed by Ledwinka, with a tubular backbone chassis, rear-mounted
engine and independent swing-axle rear suspension. The same basic
layout was used in the 1934 Model 97 Tatra, which had the enveloping
aerodynamic body which is now associated with the make. The name
Tatra is derived from the most important mountain range of
Czechoslovakia.

AMILCAR *France*

The name of the most famous small sports car to come out of France had
nothing to do with the Carthaginians. It was in fact an anagram; though
of precisely what is not known. The financial backers of the *voiturette*
that began to issue from the Paris works in 1921 were a M. Lamy and a
M. Akar, and an anagram can more or less be made from their surnames.
On the other hand, the latter's full name was Emile Akar, and if that is
said quickly, it begins to sound like 'Amilcar'. To deepen the mystery,
it has been said that the 'A's in the name on the emblem have a Masonic
connection, being in outline like the Masonic symbol that combines
dividers and a T-square. Another radiator emblem, in a shield shape,
incorporated the name of Paris.

BALLOT *France*

Before the First World War, the name Ballot was associated with engines, not motor cars. That they made marine engines is evident from the nautical nature of the car radiator emblem illustrated: the central anchor, flanked by the initials E.B. (Ernest Ballot) in red and green—the colours of a ship's port and starboard navigation lights as seen from dead ahead. Power units were also made for aircraft, motor cycles, commercial vehicles and industrial use. Engines for motor-car manufacturers who assembled their products were supplied at one time or another to Delage, Sizaire-Naudin, La Licorne, Turcat-Méry, Mass, Sigma, and many others. Ballot's first road vehicles were taxicabs, followed by racing machines in 1919, while his first passenger cars appeared two years later. The last were made in 1931, for a year before Hispano-Suiza had taken the firm over.

BERLIET *France*

One of the most famous names in the engineering city of Lyon is Berliet. It started life in 1898 in a manner that could hardly have been more humble: Marius Berliet began making cars in that year with three workmen. Backing him was Emile Lavirotte, who in 1894, with one Audibert, had made the Audibert et Lavirotte car, also in Lyon. The Berliet car was made in the old Lavirotte factory. From 1905 to 1909 the American Locomotive Company built the Berliet under licence, calling it the Alco. The association was reflected in the emblem illustrated. The words *marque déposée* mean 'registered trademark'. The firm has recently been taken over by Citroën.

BRASIER *France*

The Société du Trèfle à Quatre Feuilles offered bicycles of good quality for many years before making a car, a *voiturette* of German Benz type with a single-cylinder engine, in 1898. The designer was Georges Richard, after whom the new car was named, and it was built by the Société des Anciens Etablissements Georges Richard. In 1902 Henri Brasier, who had worked for the house of Mors from 1886 on steam and gasoline cars and boats, took charge of design. His cars were much bigger, more powerful and more modern, and these Richard-Brasiers, as they came to be called, made their name in competition, notably by winning the Gordon Bennett Trophy in 1904 and 1905. Georges Richard left in 1905, and the firm's car became known simply as Brasiers. They still carried the famous old *trèfle à quatre feuilles* (four-leafed clover) of the bicycle days. Solid, conservative design was the theme of the 1920s. In 1927, the Société des Automobiles Brasier was reorganized as the Société Chaigneau-Brasier under new control. Its products were more up-to-date cars, but the firm was too ambitious, embarking on big straight-eights with front wheel drive. It died in 1930. Aero engines were also made.

BUGATTI *France, Germany*

The Bugatti had two homes in its lifetime, because the works were at Molsheim, in Alsace—part of Germany until 1918, and restored to France thereafter. Ettore Bugatti, Italian born, built his first car in 1898. His design, after development, was taken over by De Dietrich of Niederbronn, the German branch of a famous Franco-German firm. Bugatti later designed cars for the Gasmotorenfabrik Deutz of Cologne, and E.E.C. Mathis of Strasbourg, but he achieved real fame after he began to make cars under his own name, in 1909, and more particularly after he entered racing consistently, after 1920. His beautifully-made machines were seen as luxury cars and sports cars as well as on the circuits. The basic pattern of the emblem illustrated, though not the name, was first seen on the Bugatti-designed Deutz. The monogram is formed of the intials 'EB'.

CHENARD-WALCKER *France*

The S.A. des Anciens Etablissements Chenard et Walcker were engineers before they turned to motor tricycles and quadricycles, and then to cars in 1901. E. Chenard should not be confused with Louis Chenard, who was also a car manufacturer. In its later years the firm concentrated on commercial vehicles, though passenger cars were made until 1946. It had been taken over by Chausson, and in 1951 disappeared into the maw of Peugeot. The most famous emblem of the Chenard-Walcker was the Napoleonic eagle of France, symbol of empire, courage and military prowess that had been borne at the head of Bonaparte's regiments, and before them at the head of the legions of Rome. Another emblem consisted simply of the maker's name.

CITROËN *France*

Andre Citroën's career in the motor industry went back before the First World War, when he was chief engineer of Mors. He went into the manufacture of gearwheels on his own account, and during the war, when engaged on contracts, went to America to study the new techniques of mass-production being applied to motor vehicles and other material. Citroën's factory became the biggest making shells in the whole of France. With the coming of peace, he put his experience of mass-production to work building cars for the popular market, anticipating, rightly, that there would be a boom in motoring for the masses. His 10CV of 1919 was Europe's first mass-produced car. The B12 Citroën of 1925 was the first quantity-produced European car to have an all-steel body, which was on Budd patents, while the 1934 'Traction Avant', while not the world's first mass-produced car to have front wheel drive, being beaten to that by the DKW, certainly did more to popularize this feature. The Citroën emblem is a stylization of the chevron pattern used by Citroën in his gear-cutting days.

DARRACQ *France*

Alexandre Darracq was an engineer whose first independent business was making cheap bicycles—the Gladiator, a French machine in spite of its name and being British-designed. He was very successful, but the motor vehicle was arriving on the French scene at around the same time, and Darracq determined to exploit this as well. In the interests of cheapness, he turned first to the motor cycle, and then, in 1899, acquired the rights in the latest design of the famous Léon Bollée, which had four wheels, unlike Bollée's first creation, but still used belt drive. Darracq, still anxious to find a cheap car to make in large numbers, which had to be thoroughly satisfactory and modern, soon abandoned the Darracq-Bollée and lighted upon the new Renault design, with its shaft transmission. This Darracq, which followed many features of the Renault, launched its creator as the biggest car manufacturer in France, with 1,200 being made in 1901 alone. By 1912 Darracq had retired, and the Société Alexandre Darracq, though French enough in name, had more British than French directors and capital. It gained control of the English Clément-Talbot and Sunbeam firms in 1919 and 1920 respectively, in order to make cars in Britain as well, forming the S.T.D. combine. The French-produced cars were renamed Talbot-Darracqs, but were sold from Acton in London as Darracqs (with British bodywork) to avoid confusion with the English Talbot. Soon thereafter, the name 'Darracq' was dropped in France, the French-made cars being known as Talbots. The S.T.D. combine fell apart in 1935, when Rootes took over the latter two firms. The name of Darracq was used in England, but for the wholly French made Talbot-Lago, to distinguish them from the Talbots still being built in England under Rootes control.

DELAGE *France*

Louis Delage introduced his first car, a sporting *voiturette*, in 1906, and before the First World War had gained a reputation in one of the fields in which his name was to become famous—racing—by means of wins in the 1908 Grand Prix des Voiturettes and the 1911 Coupe de *l'Auto*. During the 1920s, until the firm's retirement from racing in 1927, Delage was the premier sporting *marque* of France, winning the French Grand Prix and the British Grand Prix twice, and carrying off the World's Land Speed Record once. In the same era, it also became known for its fast luxury cars, which survived up to 1954. From 1935, Delage was under Delahaye control.

DE DION-BOUTON *France*

In 1883 Count Albert De Dion, Georges Bouton and a M. Trépardoux
started to build steam road vehicles, De Dion providing the finance and
Bouton and Trépardoux the technical skills. De Dion began to investigate
the possibilities of gasoline vehicles ten years afterwards, at first making
them alongside his steamers, to the disgust of Trépardoux, who quit the
firm. De Dion's first gasoline engine was made in 1895, and motor
tricycles were his first vehicles so powered. A quadricycle followed, and
a car proper in 1899. The engines were remarkable for their day
because of their high rate of revolutions, which gave them an
exceptionally high power-to-weight ratio. De Dion's first car also
incorporated the De Dion axle design, whereby the drive was
transmitted to the rear wheels by shafts independent of the axle, which
was carried separately. Later, in 1910, De Dion became the first firm to
put a vee-eight engine into series production. The last passenger cars
were built in 1932. The emblem shown here features a winged wheel
with the words *marque déposée* (registered trademark) and the name of
the car on its rim, and below, the address of the works: 12 rue Ernest,
Puteaux, Seine. The significance of the letters LABC on the spokes of
the wheel is not known. It is possible that they should be read 'L'ABC',
meaning that the De Dion was as simple as that, or that it had been in
the industry since the beginning, or that it was all that could be desired.

DELAHAYE *France*

Emile Delahaye founded Delahaye et Cie in 1893–4, becoming, in the
latter year, one of the earliest French motor manufacturers. Like so many
others, he started with a vehicle based on the successful German Benz.
From the beginning, Delahayes were solid, conventional cars, lacking in
any sort of *panache* until the arrival of the sporting Type 135 in 1936. This
was the Delahaye which made the name famous on a worldwide scale.
Gasoline engines for various uses, taxicabs and commercial vehicles were
also made at different times. In its last years, the Delage, by the 1950s a
very similar car, was built in the Delahaye works. The initials G.F.A.
appearing on the emblem stand for Société *Generale Française* de
Construction *Automobile*, this being the consortium set up in 1942 to
pool the sales efforts of Delahaye, Delage, Simca, and three truck
concerns.

DELAUNAY-BELLEVILLE *France*

The S.A. des Automobiles Delaunay-Belleville was the motor manufacturing branch of a famous engineering firm specializing in marine boilers. Like their other products, the cars were beautifully built and finished, earning the title of the Rolls-Royce of France. From the first car of 1904 until the late 1920s, the Delaunay-Belleville wore a round radiator that recalled the parent company's boilers. Otherwise, it was conventional enough, though luxurious and expensive in the extreme. It was the Tsar of Russia's favourite. There was a long jump from these cars to the commonplace American-engined Delaunays of 1930, to the R16 of 1938 with all-independent suspension, and to the Rovin baby car made by the company after the Second World War.

HOTCHKISS *France*

The crossed gunbarrels of the Hotchkiss emblem, a shell with burning fuse between them, were an indication of the company's origins as an armaments manufacturer. Hotchkiss was an American who provided the Emperor Napoleon III with munitions during the Franco-Prussian War of 1870–1, including the *mitrailleuse*, one of the first machine-guns. Hotchkiss became noted for their quick-firing light artillery and machine-guns. However, the S.A. des Anciens Etablissements Hotchkiss et Cie was in decline when, at the works of the latter company at St Denis, the first Hotchkiss cars were built in 1903. They soon established a fine reputation for quality, and saved the firm. Parts for other motor manufacturers were also made. Henceforth, the emphasis was on cars. They pioneered the Hotchkiss drive, in which the torque of the open propeller shaft was taken by the rear springs. The last Hotchkiss cars were made in 1955.

TALBOT-LAGO *France*

The Sunbeam-Talbot-Darracq combine, which had made Sunbeams and English Talbots in Britain and French Talbots in France, was the result of the acquisition in 1919–20 by the French Darracq concern (a firm under British control in spite of its name) of the English Clément-Talbot and Sunbeam companies. The French Talbots were made by Automobiles Talbot, the French 'end' of S.T.D. Their cars were called Darracqs in England, to avoid confusion with the English Talbot. This complicated set-up disintegrated when in 1935 Clément-Talbot were taken over by Rootes, and Sunbeam, after going into receivership, went the same way. Major A. F. Lago, head of Automobiles Talbot of Suresnes, the last survivor, began in 1936 to make competition cars of extremely high performance known as Talbot-Lagos. They could be, and were, used in both sports-car and Grand Prix racing. They were still called Darracqs in Britain.

LORRAINE-DIETRICH *France, Germany*

The De Dietrich firm was founded in the reign of Louis XIV. By 1896 De Dietrich et Cie were well-known manufacturers of railway rolling-stock and equipment who, in 1896, began tentatively to enter motor manufacture. First the Baron de Turckheim, head of the firm and a member of an old Alsace family, asked Amédée Bollée to make him a car; but this was obsolescent by 1900, and he now went to the brothers-in-law Turcat and Méry who were making cars in Marseilles on Daimler lines. At around the same time, the company also built some cars of the Belgian Vivinus type. In other words, De Dietrich, like so many other pioneers, were looking for a good existing car rather than designing one themselves. They found a satisfactory answer in the Turcat-Méry, which, however, was soon modified as the De Dietrich. Ettore Bugatti was employed as consultant designer by the company's German factory at Niederbronn. There was also a works at Lunéville in Lorraine and, a little later, at Argenteuil, Seine et Oise. In 1905 the cars were renamed Lorraine-Dietrich. The cross of Lorraine, with its distinctive double crosspiece, is attributed to the great family of Guise, who ruled over the Duchy of Lorraine from the beginning of the sixteenth century. From the time of the First World War, aero engines as well as cars were built, all the latter now being French, and going out of production in 1935.

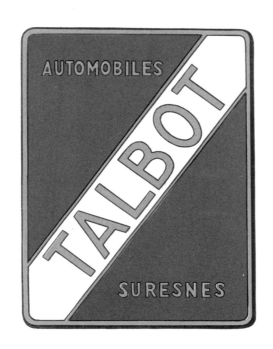

AUTOMOBILES TALBOT SURESNES

63

MORS *France*

Initially, Emile Mors was an electrical engineer first and a maker of motor cars second, as the name of his company, the Société d'Electricité et d'Automobiles Mors, suggests. The firm had been founded in 1851. Its earliest car, of 1896, was a Benz derivative like so many of its contemporaries, but in 1897 there appeared an original design with a vee-four engine and low-tension magneto ignition. Mors was the pioneer of the earliest successful car dynamo, seen on this car. The engine design did not last long, and Mors, under the technical direction of Henri Brasier and later of André Citroën, became best known for fast, well-made, modern but conventional machines. These were made until 1927, latterly under Citroën control. During the Second World War, from 1941 to 1943, a brief return was made to car production with a miniature electric vehicle designed to combat the fuel shortage. The shape of the emblem shown is that of the Mors radiator, and dates from the years immediately before 1914.

PANHARD-LEVASSOR *France*

René Panhard and Emile Levassor made woodworking machinery, and from 1887 built the German Daimler engine under licence in France for Edouard Sarazin, holders of the licence for France. A complete Daimler car was shown at the Paris Exhibition of 1889, and a year later Panhard et Levassor made their own first complete vehicle round the Panhard-built engine. It closely resembled its German parent, but a year later appeared a native design that made the name of Panhard-Levassor for ever famous: a front-mounted engine, driving to the rear wheels via a friction-type clutch and sliding-pinion gearbox. This was the basic layout of the modern car—the Panhard-Levassor's chain drive was the only fundamental difference, and by 1898 Renault had introduced shaft drive with a direct top gear. The linked initials PL are those of the makers, while on the emblem illustrated there also appears 'SS'. This stands for 'Sans Soupapes'—without valves. Strictly, 'sleeve valves' would be more exact. From 1912 the Knight-type double sleeve-valve engine was introduced into the Panhard range, and for several years after 1922, no others were to be had from the firm.

65

PEUGEOT *France*

Les Fils de Peugeot Frères, makers of saw blades and spring leaves, began to build bicycles in 1885, and three years later Armand Peugeot's first motor car appeared; the three-wheeled steamer of 1890, fitted with a Serpollet engine. It was never put into serious production. The earliest Peugeot to achieve this status was a gasoline car that first saw the light in 1891, and had a Panhard-Levassor engine of German Daimler origin. One line of models in the early 1900s were known as Lion-Peugeots. The lion of this range, that came to be the emblem of all Peugeots, to some extent represents the Lion of Belfort, the monument that commemorates the defence of the city of Belfort against the Germans in 1871. Its sculptor, Bartholdi, was also responsible for the Statue of Liberty in New York harbour. The Peugeot factories are grouped in the vicinity of Belfort; hence the adoption of the lion. In addition, the province of Franche-Comté in which is situated Montbéliard, where Peugeots are made, has a lion in its arms.

RENAULT *France*

The Renault brothers gave to the motor car the transmission layout which is still used by most of the world's models—there was direct drive on top gear, and power was transmitted not through the customary chains or combination of belts and chains, but through a universally-jointed shaft. Their first car appeared in 1898; five years later, the 'trademark' that distinguished Renaults externally, and was to be widely copied, appeared: the dashboard-mounted radiator with 'coal-scuttle' hood in front. The Renault 'diamond' is therefore not strictly a 'radiator' emblem, but one worn on the hood. An electric horn was fitted inside the latter, and from 1922 a hole was cut in it to allow the sound to escape. This hole was covered by a round metal grille with the word 'Renault' on a band across the grille. Two years later, the grille became diamond-shaped. The diamond has remained long after it ceased to be a grille.

SALMSON *France*

The Société des Moteurs Salmson of Billancourt started life by making liquid-cooled aero engines. Emile Salmson had been experimenting with a seven-cylinder radial unit as early as 1909, with one pushrod per cylinder like most of the Salmsons of the 1920s, but had no success until he received the backing of Messrs Canton and Unie. Thereafter, and during the First World War, aero engines were built, but by 1919 the company was offering the GN cyclecar from Britain under licence. The step had been logical: there was a slump in the aviation business following the end of wartime orders, and many firms in the aero industry turned to cars. It was sensible to adopt an already tried and tested design. However, by 1921 Salmson were already making their own double overhead-camshaft four-cylinder engine fitted into a GN frame. Machines based on this design were very difficult to beat in small-car racing. The more touring Salmsons had four push-and-pull rods and four rockers for the eight valves. In the 1930s and on until car production ended in 1955, the small sporting Salmson gave way to more sedate fast touring machines. All were designed by Emil Petit. The emblem of the 1920s featured the monogram letters SMS, the initials of the firm's name. The words 'Syst. Canton Unie' refer to Salmson's original backers.

SIMCA *France*

Henri-Theodore Pigozzi was a Piedmontese who came to France to make his fortune in 1924, setting himself up as a scrap metal merchant. His metal went to the Fiat steel mills in Turin. By 1926 Pigozzi was the Fiat distributor for France, and two years later was assembling Fiats at Suresnes. In 1934, the S.A. des Automobiles Donnet of Nanterre went out of business, and Pigozzi bought their factory in order to expand his activities. He founded the Société Industrielle de Mécanique et de Carrosserie Automobile (SIMCA), and from now on, although his products continued to be French Fiats, they were made under the name of Simca. The Simca Cinq and Simca Huit, which were mechanically the Fiat 500 and 1100 respectively, were a great success, and by 1939 2,000 cars a month were being turned out. In 1951 their best-known model, the Aronde, was launched. It was the first Simca to show independence of Turin. The name was the old French word for the swallow, of which a stylized version appeared on the Simca emblem shown here. This emblem was dropped after Simca became a member of the Chrysler group, when the latter's star emblem was adopted.

SIZAIRE-NAUDIN *France*

The Sizaire-Naudin, whose initials appear on the pennant in the emblem illustrated, was one of the first of the inexpensive, simple, sporting small cars with one, two, and later four cylinders for which France became famous between around 1905 and the late 1920s. The Etablissements Sizaire et Naudin took their name from Maurice Sizaire, the designer of the car, and the Naudin brothers, who built it. The machine's most notable features were its independent front suspension, and its direct drive on all three forward speeds by means of a movable ring on the propeller shaft engaging different sets of teeth in the final drive. By 1914, however, the Sizaire-Naudin was a conventional car, and remained so until its death in 1921. Sizaire had departed in 1913 to design the Sizaire-Berwick, a normal luxury car that had a French chassis and was made under the auspices of F. W. Berwick, the British agents for Sizaire-Naudin. Afterwards Sizaire went on to design another highly original machine, the Sizaire-Frères, which had all-independent suspension—the world's first production car to use this feature. The other set of initials on the emblem shown, C.J.L., stands for Charles Jarrott & Letts Ltd, the predecessors of F. W. Berwick as British agents for the make. Not all these cars had an emblem.

UNIC *France*

Until 1905 Georges Richard made the successful small car that bore his name. In that year, he left to make the Unic, so called because it was to be either the fruit of a single-model policy, as has been suggested, or else simply unique. The latter seems to be the more likely explanation, as there were three models within a year. Georges Richard's new product never became as famous as the old, remaining one of the less well-known solid French touring cars of the 1920s and 1930s. From 1939, only trucks were built. The emblem illustrated bears George Richard's name, and that of the Paris suburb where his and so many other cars were made: Puteaux.

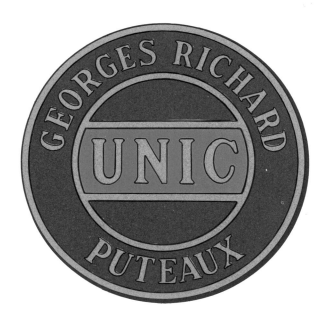

VOISIN *France*

Gabriel Voisin the engineer was better known for his aircraft before and during the First World War than for the cars that he made after it. He was one of the most important early pioneers of the heavier-than-air craft, and, indeed, claimed to have flown a practical aeroplane before the Wright brothers. This depends on what one means by 'flown'. He went over to cars when peace came, like so many other aircraft manufacturers, taking over an unused Citroën design to do so. This had a double sleeve-valve engine of Knight type. So did all succeeding Voisins, until the last ones, which used American Graham engines. Voisin had other loves as well. One was the abolition of gear-changing, which led to multi-cylinder engines, experiments with infinitely variable gears and the standardization of the Cotal electric gearbox on some models. Weight reduction was another enthusiasm, giving rise to many light patent bodies in wood and aluminium, of unsurpassed ugliness. Voisin's originality extended to his emblem, the Egyptian scarab, which was also worn by his aircraft. The scarab was a symbol in the form of a beetle, and was sacred to the sun-god. It appeared in Egyptian religion with outstretched wings as representing the vivifying soul.

ADLER *Germany*

Heinrich Kleyer began making his Adler bicycles in Frankfurt in 1886. He turned to cars in 1899, like so many German manufacturers taking up a French licence; in his case that of De Dion-Bouton. Motor cycles were also made, as well as typewriters and aero engines. As the first decade of the new century wore on, Adler became best known for big, powerful cars of conventional design. Only one Adler was a notable exception in this period: the engineer Edmund Rumpler, later to be famous, in 1903 designed one with swing-axle independent suspension and unit construction of engine and gearbox. Production models were unexciting enough, until the arrival of the Trumpf model of 1932, with front wheel drive and independent suspension, designed by H. G. Röhr. The emblem, shown here, is a very stylized eagle—*Adler* in German means eagle.

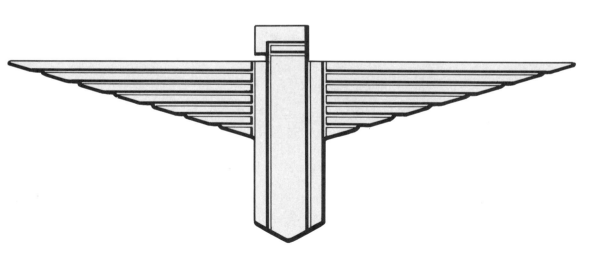

AUDI *Germany*

Dr August Horch, founder of the Horch Werke of Zwickau, lost control of his creation in 1909, but established a new marque, the Audi. Its name, meaning 'hear!' in Latin, was a literal translation of the German word *horch*. The first Audi was made in 1910, and the make quickly made a name for itself in competition, as had the Horch. Financial difficulties in the 1920s led to J. S. Rasmussen of D.K.W. gaining control in 1928. A complete change of design to the popular American type of car followed— big but cheap. Some used the American Rickenbacker engine. The firm, together with D.K.W., Horch and Wanderer, became a part of the Auto- Union consortium in 1932. From 1934 until 1939 the Audi-Front was the make's offering, with front-wheel drive. The Audi-Front was made in the Horch factory, while the D.K.W. was built by Audi. Some emblems incorporated the four linked circles of Auto-Union, symbolizing the four united manufacturers. The Audi name has been revived since 1965 by the Auto-Union GmbH.

B.M.W. *Germany*

The Bayerische Motoren Werke was founded in 1916, and made aero engines for military purposes. After the coming of peace they went on to manufacture engines for trucks and boats, and twin-cylinder air-cooled engines for motor cycles and the then-popular cyclecars. From 1923 they began to build complete motor cycles, that have become world- famous. The firm also made four-cylinder motor car engines of advanced design, but their first car came about as a result of the B.M.W. takeover in 1928 of the Fahrzeugfabrik Eisenach, who a year earlier had begun to make the Austin Seven from Britain under licence, as the Dixi. It was now renamed B.M.W., and improved in appearance. The B.M.W. emblem arose from their aviation work. It represents, in highly stylized form, the circle described by a rotating airscrew, the blue being the sky.

BORGWARD *Germany*

The complicated history of the origins of the Borgward begins in 1905, when the Hansa Automobil Gesellschaft began making cars at Varel in Oldenburg. A year later, in Bremen, Dr Heinrich Weigand of the Norddeutscher Lloyd shipping company launched the Norddeutsche Automobil und Motoren A.G. The NAMAG bore the name Lloyd on its radiator. Some Lloyds had front-wheel drive. The two firms amalgamated in 1914, to form the Hansa-Lloyd Werke A.G. This firm made cars under the name of Hansa-Lloyd in Bremen. At the same time, Hansas continued to appear, made by the Hansa Automobilwerke A.G. in Varel. In 1929, both firms, suffering from the Depression, came under the protective wing of Borgward & Tecklenborg, together with the Goliath Werke, makers of three-wheelers. No more Hansa-Lloyds were made after 1929, but the Hansa continued until 1938. Four years before, the new group was named the Hansa-Lloyd-und-Goliath Werke, making the Hansa and the Goliath in Bremen. It was renamed the Carl F.W. Borgward GmbH in 1938, and in the following year the first Borgward car appeared. This was made until 1961. From 1949 until the same year, a new member of the group, the Lloyd Maschinenfabrik GmbH also built the Lloyd economy car alongside the Borgward. The red and white colours of the Borgward emblem go back to the Hansa-Lloyd car, which used them because red and silver featured in the city arms of Bremen.

D.K.W. *Germany*

In 1921 Jorgen Skafte Rasmussen started to make 25 c.c. engines for power-assisted bicycles, then went on to motor cycles proper. The first D.K.W. motor car (the initials stood for Deutsche Kraftfahrtzeug Werke AG) appeared in 1928; an original and modern design with a two-stroke engine and integral body-chassis construction. Three years later came D.K.W.'s most famous design, the front-wheel drive, two-cylinder car. In 1932 D.K.W., Audi, Horch and Wanderer were joined in the Auto-Union consortium. The four cars continued to be made under their own names; at this time, the only machine to be made as an Auto-Union was the famous Grand Prix racing car. The first three names died, but from 1949 a new company, Auto-Union GmbH, continued to make the D.K.W. The emblem illustrated combines the badge of D.K.W. with the four linked circles representing the makes originally comprising Auto-Union. Some models were renamed Auto-Union in 1958, but by 1966 D.K.W. was again the only name in use. From 1965 the company has also made the new Audi, resurrecting an old name.

HORCH *Germany*

Dr August Horch of Zwickau in Saxony worked for Benz at Mannheim, then set up his own company in 1899, to make engines. He built his first cars in 1903, starting with small, rather commonplace vehicles, but very soon coming to concentrate on big, fast and expensive cars, for which they were famous. In 1926, Paul Daimler, late head of the company bearing his name, introduced the Type 300 series Horch with eight cylinders in line, that was probably the make's best known model. The emblem illustrated comes from one of these cars. The most spectacular Horch was certainly the vee-twelve, current from 1932 until 1936. The company was joined with Audi, Wanderer and DKW in the Auto-Union consortium in 1932. Its last cars were made in 1938.

MERCEDES-BENZ *Germany*

In 1901, the Daimler Motoren Gesellschaft, one of the world's first motor manufacturers, made a specially powerful and modern car for Emil Jellinek, an Austrian businessman-*cum*-diplomat, who had entered races under the pseudonym of Herr Mercedes, this being his daughter's name. Compared with its contemporaries it had a longer chassis and lower centre of gravity. There were combined for the first time in one car mechanically-operated inlet valves, a honeycomb radiator, gate gear-change and pressed-steel frame. It was to be called the Mercedes-type Daimler in several European countries and the United States. 'Mercedes' soon became the only name by which it was known. It was the most famous car of its day, and was copied everywhere from its earliest times. Carl Benz made his first car in 1886. Cheap, simple, reliable machines based on modifications of the first Benz design developed into the world's first approximation to a popular, quantity-produced car: the Benz Velo. The interests and resources of Daimler and of Benz were united in 1925, in the Daimler-Benz AG. After 1926, the separate Mercedes and Benz marques were discontinued in favour of the Mercedes-Benz. The three-pointed star of the emblem had been adopted by Daimler in 1909 as their trademark. The house of the late Gottlieb Daimler, who had given the company its name, had borne a star, and the father had told his son Paul, now in charge, that 'a star shall arise from here, and I hope that it will bring blessings to us and to our children'. The laurel wreath in the emblem was the trademark of Benz. The star enclosed by a wreath was used as a symbol of the union of the two firms from 1926 to 1937, when the plain ring and star now current were adopted.

N.S.U. *Germany*

The Neckarsulmer Fahrzeugwerke, from which name the initials N.S.U.
come, started life in 1873 making knitting machines. From 1880 they
went on to bicycles and motor cycles. The first N.S.U. motor car was
built in 1906; it was the Pipe from Belgium, made under licence.
Nowadays the company, renamed the N.S.U. Motorenwerke A.G., still
offers a car of foreign extraction, as well as home-grown designs, only
now its origin is Fiat of Italy. This has been the case since 1929. The
shield-shaped emblem bears the town arms of Neckarsulm beneath
the name N.S.U. To the left are heraldic stag's antlers, part of the arms
of the former kingdom of Württemberg, while on their right is the cross
of the knights of the Teutonic Order, who had a castle at Neckarsulm in
the Middle Ages. The Teutonic Knights were a German military order
founded for service in the Holy Land. After the fall of the Latin
Kingdom of Jerusalem, they settled in East Prussia, where they engaged
in frontier campaigns against the Poles and Russians.

OPEL *Germany*

The name of Opel first appeared on sewing-machines in 1862, and next
on bicycles. In 1898 the earliest Opel car arrived. This was based on
the Lutzmann design, a primitive machine that had been current since
1894 and had been taken over and improved by Opel. From 1900, Opel
made the Darracq car from France under licence; the first car designed
by Opel themselves did not appear until 1902. Although they came in all
sizes, Opels before the First World War were already providing
Germany's nearest approximation to a car with mass appeal, the
Puppchen (Doll), and were the country's biggest car producer. In 1924
they became the first to adopt mass production techniques, with the
Laubfrosch (Tree Frog), which was the French 5CV Citroën built under
licence. General Motors took over in 1928. The emblem illustrated, now
worn by Opel passenger cars, originated in the Opel Blitz truck. It was
called the Blitz (Lightning) because it was exceptionally fast, and the
streak of lightning is shown in the emblem.

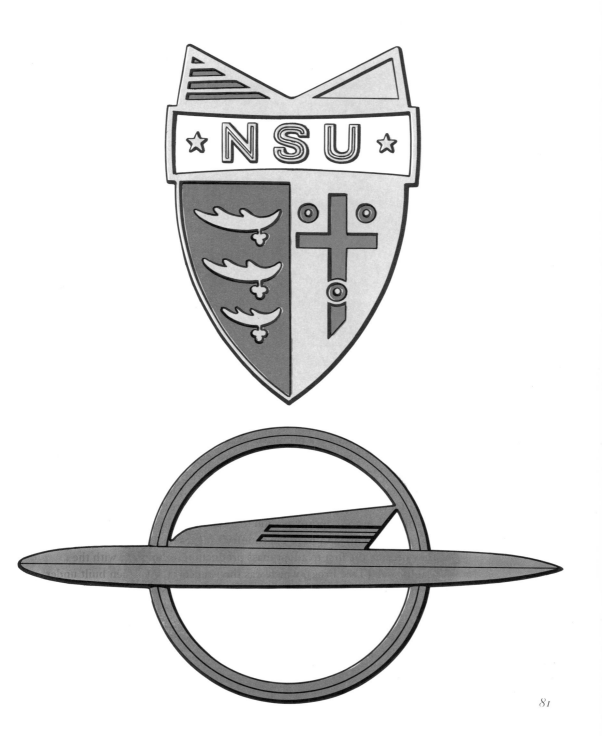

PORSCHE *Germany*

The Porsche, Germany's most famous modern sporting make, is named after Ferry Porsche, son of the Austrian designer Ferdinand Porsche, who had been responsible in the 1930s for the Auto-Union racing car and the Volkswagen. After the Second World War, Ferry Porsche continued the firm of consulting engineers that his father had founded, developing the advanced and efficient Porsche sports car from the Volkswagen design. Horses have formed part of the arms of Stuttgart, where the Porsche is made, since the Middle Ages, when the town was founded on the site of a stud farm—hence the name. The stag's antlers and red and black stripes in the quarterings of the shield are part of the arms of the former kingdom of Württemberg.

VOLKSWAGEN *Germany*

The world-famous Volkswagen or People's Car had its origins in the KDF-Wagen laid down in 1934, a Third Reich state project of which the prototypes were built by N.S.U. The first production cars were not made until 1939. The Volkswagen emblem represents the crest of the town of Wolfsburg, where the car's main factory was located. The town was named after a nearby castle, the name of which means the 'Wolf's Castle', which accounts for the stylized wolf and castle on the emblem. Nowadays the latter is no longer found in so prominent a place as the trunk lid of the Volkswagen, because the car is made in many different places.

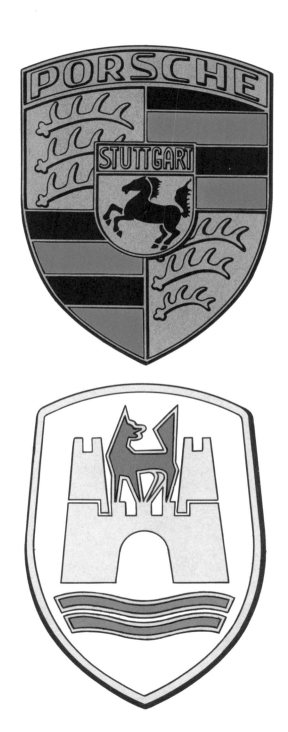

WANDERER *Germany*

The Wanderer of Schoenau-Chemnitz started life as a bicycle in 1885.
Motor cycles were made from 1902, and acquired a fine reputation.
Around 1911, the firm acquired the right to use Bugatti patents in
Germany, and launched into production of a very modern, well-made,
expensive small car. This first Wanderer car was peculiar in that its
standard body was a tandem two-seater, later supplemented by a three-
seater 'cloverleaf' layout. This type was dropped after 1925, after which
Wanderers became conventional, following American lines, until 1932.
Then Ferdinand Porsche produced a Wanderer with swing-axle
independent rear suspension, and a year later the firm was absorbed into
the Auto-Union consortium, with D.K.W., Audi and Horch. The last
Wanderers were made in 1939.

DAF *Holland*

The initials DAF stand for Van Doorne's Automobielfabrieken N.V.,
the only firm of any significance making passenger cars of Dutch origin
today. The brothers Hub and Wim van Doorne went into the
automotive repair business in 1928. Two years later they began to make
trailers and semi-trailers. They enjoyed great success with their Trado
unit of 1935, designed to convert four-wheeled, two-wheel-drive trucks
into six-wheelers with four-wheel drive for cross-country use. This was
incorporated in the DAF armoured car and amphibious military vehicle
of 1938. From 1948 buses and then trucks were built, and the company's
first passenger car, with fully automatic transmission of epicyclic type,
appeared in 1959.

SPYKER *Holland*

H. J. Spyker made cars from 1900 in a factory at Trompenburg near Amsterdam. The make that bore his name was Holland's only major representative in the industry apart from DAF. The last Spykers were built in 1925, by which time they had become expensive luxury cars, of modern design (as always). The radiator emblem illustrated was designed by Henri Wijnmalen, General Manager of the Spyker works from 1914 to 1922. The wire wheel, of course, represents the motor car, while the airscrew is a reflection of the company's simultaneous interest in aero engines and aircraft. Wijnmalen himself had been an aviator. The Latin motto beneath, freely translated, means 'Nothing is insuperable to the tenacious'. The emblem was used on all the post-First World War models.

ABARTH *Italy*

This car with the un-Italian name was in fact the creation of an Austrian, Carl Abarth. He first came to Italy in 1947, with Ing. Hruska, an agent for Ferry Porsche's design consultancy, to work for Dusio at Cisitalia on the Porsche-designed Cisitalia Grand Prix car. When Dusio and Cisitalia failed through making cars that were too expensive, Abarth stayed in Italy to make motor components, and become famous for the performance he extracted from Fiat engines of various sizes. He made cars of his own based on Fiat components, that have carried his scorpion emblem. Its origin is simple: Carl Abarth was born under the zodiacal sign of Scorpio.

ALFA ROMEO *Italy*

In 1906 the Frenchman Alexandre Darracq began to make taxicabs in Portello, a district of Milan, but within four years had sold out to the Societa Anonima Lombarda Fabbrica Automobili, who began a car of native design called the A.L.F.A. In 1914, Nicola Romeo became manager of the firm, and its name was changed to the Societa Anonima Ing. N. Romeo. After the First World War, its cars were renamed Alfa Romeo. Their emblem includes, in the left-hand segment of the inside circle, a cross; and in the right-hand segment, a crowned serpent with a human figure in its mouth. These two symbols form the arms of the city of Milan, which were also the arms of the Visconti Dukes of Milan. According to one story, the cross dates from the time of the First Crusade (1095–9), in which Milanese recruits took part, the cross being that of the Crusaders. The serpent has had half a dozen origins attributed to it. The human figure is said variously to be a child, and a defeated Saracen added after the Crusade.

BIANCHI *Italy*

The Societa Anonima Edoardo Bianchi was founded in 1885 by its namesake. In 1899 Bianchi and Gianfranco Tommaselli, a racing cyclist, went into partnership to make cars as well as bicycles, under the name of the S.A. Automobili e Velocipedi Edoardo Bianchi. Their first machines were small economy cars, but they soon branched out into making solid, orthodox vehicles for the middle-class market. Trucks and buses were built too, and bicycle manufacture was continued, and in the 1920s and early 1930s, all types of car were offered, from a small car to a big straight-eight. Car production ceased in 1938, to be resumed after an interval of nineteen years building the other lines, with the Bianchina, which was Fiat-based. The Autobianchi Primula of 1965 owed a great deal to the British BMC Mini. The emblem shown features the cross of Savoy, of which kingdom Milan, where the car was built, once formed part. The heraldic eagle is that of the Visconti, Dukes of Milan for most of the Middle Ages, and it also figures (by marriage) on the arms of the Sforzas, the Viscontis' successors.

FERRARI *Italy*

Enzo Ferrari gained his earliest experience of the motor industry with the otherwise long-forgotten C.M.N. concern (Costruzione Meccaniche Nazionali), becoming one of its works competition drivers. He then worked for Alfa Romeo in the same capacity, in 1929 forming the Scuderia Ferrari, the unofficial works team founded when the company withdrew from racing. The Alfa Romeo of the Scuderia Ferrari wore the famous prancing horse emblem. This had first been borne by the fighter aircraft of the Italian First World War ace Francesco Baracca. Ferrari had met Baracca's parents after the war in which the hero died, and they had persuaded him to adopt the flying horse as his own mascot. The horse was always black. The gold of the field is the colour of Modena, the town in which the Scuderia Ferrari Alfa Romeos were prepared, and in which have been made the post-Second World War Ferrari racing and sports cars to which Ferrari turned after Alfa Romeo resumed control of their works team in 1938.

FIAT *Italy*

The Fiat name was originally rendered F.I.A.T., being the initials of the company that manufactured it, the Fabbricca Italiana Automobili Torino. In 1899 Giovanni Agnelli offered his first F.I.A.T., a car based on the Welleyes, a make Agnelli had acquired to gain experience. F.I.A.T. very quickly became the biggest motor manufacturing concern in Italy, and has never lost that distinction. The car's name was changed to Fiat in 1906. The significance of the laurel wreath surrounding the name on the emblem is uncertain, but it was a common device on car emblems, and may have stood for achievement. This emblem was used from about 1922 to around 1931, coming in with the squarish radiator that replaced the original oval radiator, which bore an oval badge. It was dropped with the coming of grilles to the Fiat range, when a new emblem was cast into the grille.

ISOTTA-FRASCHINI *Italy*

Cesare Isotta and Vincenzo Fraschini were the founders of the company bearing their name. They started in 1899 by selling and then assembling the French Renault in Milan; next they made their own cars under their own name. Their most famous were the Tipo 8 and its successors the 8A, 8B and 8C, which were in turn the company's sole model from 1919 until car production ended thirty years later. The emblem shown was first fitted to the Tipo 8A in 1926, and was carried also by the Tipo 8B up to its demise around 1935. The earlier Tipo 8 had borne a circular badge enclosed by a laurel wreath with the type designation beneath it. The Tipo 8C carried the initials 'IF' alone. They are said to stand not only for Isotta-Fraschini but also for Intrepida Fides; courage and loyalty.

ITALA *Italy*

Matteo, one of the prolific Ceirano family who launched so many of Italy's car makes in the early years of the century, was responsible for the Itala. His first machine, which came in 1903, was an economy car with a French De Dion engine, but then he went over to copying the big, fast, and expensive Mercedes from Germany, as did so many Italian and other car manufacturers. The Itala soon became one of Italy's most popular makes, and, with Fiat and Isotta-Fraschini, one of the 'big three' of her manufacturers. The name Itala is a romantic, patriotic form of 'Italy', and is used as a girl's name. It suited the mood of Italy at the time when Matteo Ceirano gave it to his new car.

LANCIA *Italy*

Vincenzo Lancia, together with Giovanni Ceirano, worked on the Welleyes car that was taken over by Agnelli in 1899 as the basis of the first Fiat. Lancia went on to work for Agnelli, making his name as a racing driver for Fiat before setting up as a manufacturer on his own account in 1908. His first car was in fact made in the Itala factory, his own works having been destroyed by fire. A succession of very well-made, expensive, and conventional vehicles, each named after a letter of the alphabet (Alfa, Beta, Gamma, Delta, Epsilon, Eta, Theta, Kappa), followed until 1922, when the Lambda appeared. This was an extremely advanced design that quickly became Italy's most famous car, with its independent front suspension and unit construction of chassis and body. In its own day, the Aprilia model of the late 1930s set the standard for the small, popular car in terms of performance, roadholding and modernity, while the elegant Aurelia B20 GT was surely one of the most handsome cars ever built. The Lancia emblem was designed by Count Carlo Biscaretti di Ruffia, one of Italy's foremost motoring pioneers, and consisted of a standard mounted on a lance—providing the play on Lancia's name—superimposed on a four-spoked steering wheel complete with its knurled throttle control on the right-hand spoke. The latter was dropped from the Flaminia model of 1956.

MASERATI *Italy*

There were five Maserati brothers—Carlo, Bindo, Alfieri, Mario, Ettore and Ernesto—and all but one were involved in the motor industry. Carlo was the first to build a car, the Carcano, in 1897, then went on to work for Fiat, Bianchi and others. Bindo and Alfieri went to Isotta-Fraschini as testers. Alfieri set up independently during the First World War as a manufacturer of sparking plugs, but from 1922 concentrated on developing the Diatto car for competitions. When Diatto gave up racing, the Maserati brothers, including the youngest, Ernesto, brought out the first car to bear their own name. Then and henceforth, only racing and sports-racing machines were built. In 1948, after ten years of control by outside finance, Bindo, Ernesto and Ettore left the company bearing their name to make the O.S.C.A. The trident that has always been a feature of the Maserati emblem is a traditional symbol of the city where the cars were made, Bologna.

O.M. *Italy*

The name O.M., once found on one of Italy's most famous sports cars, was formed by the initials of the Societa Anonima Officine Meccaniche, which meant simply the Mechanical Workshops Company. The firm was established in Milan in 1899 by the fusion of A. Grondona Conic, carriage builders, with Miani Silvestri, railroad locomotive manufacturers. The new firm of O.M. came to concentrate on engines, steam and gasoline, as well as locomotives. In 1918 they acquired the Züst car and factory, and started to make motor cars under their own name, at first based on the Züst. An O.M. won the Mille Miglia race round Italy in 1927, but in that year the company also started to make trucks (the Swiss Saurer under licence). Passenger-car production ceased in 1931, and thereafter only commercial vehicles were built. Since 1933, O.M. has been part of the Fiat concern.

OSCA *Italy*

The name Osca is composed of the initials O.S.C.A., standing for Officine Specializzate Costruzione Automobili. The make was launched in 1948 by the brothers Ettore, Bindo and Ernesto Maserati—the *fratelli Maserati* on the emblem—from their small works in Bologna. Earlier, the brothers had worked for the Officine Alfieri Maserati, which before and after their departure were famous for their racing cars. For ten years before they left, however, the family firm had been run by Count Orsi, who had obtained financial control, leaving the brothers in the status of employees. They quit to regain their independence, making their sports and racing Oscas in very small numbers. The shield in the centre of the emblem forms the arms of the town of Bologna, their new home.

DATSUN *Japan*

Masujiro Hashimoto was one of Japan's earliest pioneers of the automobile industry, who in 1911 began to make cars in a Tokyo factory. His first successful design appeared in 1913—earlier ones had been inhibited by, among other drawbacks, lack of suitable materials and techniques in Japan. Indeed, the 1913 car incorporated many imported parts. The car was given the name D.A.T., from the initials of its three principal backers. In 1926 the Jitsuyo Company, who had made the Gorham three- and four-wheeler, acquired the name D.A.T. and produced a 500 c.c. two-seater under that name in 1929. With the success of the British Austin Seven, it was made under licence in Japan as the Datson. This became the Datsun in 1932. In 1935, it was taken over by the Nissan Automobile Company of Yokohama and turned out in mass quantities as Japan's first popular car. The D in the emblem is the initial of the name. The Nissan Company also makes trucks, and at one time made passenger cars under its own name as well.

MAZDA *Japan*

The Toyo Kogyo company of Hiroshima was founded in 1920 to make cork products, and entered the engineering field in 1928. A single-cylinder, three-wheeled truck appeared in 1931, followed by a car of similar design four years later. The name of Mazda was partly a play on the name of the firm's founder, Matsuda, and also stood for Ahura Mazda, the supreme god, Lord of Light, in the religious system of the Persian sage Zoroaster (sixth-seventh centuries B.C.). The Mazda passenger car in its present, conventional form dates from 1960. A year later, an agreement was made with NSU of Germany for joint development of the revolutionary Wankel engine. The emblem forms a stylized M, for Mazda.

PRINCE *Japan*

The Prince was a product of the growth of Japan's passenger-car industry after the Second World War. In 1947 a division of the Tachikawa Aircraft Company formed the Tokyo Electric Car Company to make the Tama electric car, designed to cope with the fuel shortage. The company was renamed the Tama Electric Car Company in 1949, becoming the Tama Automobile Company two years later. In 1952 it produced the first Prince gasoline car. Renamed the Prince Motor Company, the firm merged in 1954 with the Fuji Precision Machinery Company that had made its engines. Prince Motors Ltd was formed in 1961.

TOYOTA *Japan*

The Toyota Automatic Loom Factory began experiments with cars in 1933. The first prototypes were completed by 1935—the Model A-1 Toyota passenger car and the Model G-1 truck. The Toyota Motor Company was set up two years later, and in 1938 the main factory was opened. From 1947 to 1953, the only passenger cars built were taxis, but late in the latter year, the Toyopet Super appeared. The C emblem with a central star stands for Corona, a model which was first offered in 1957.

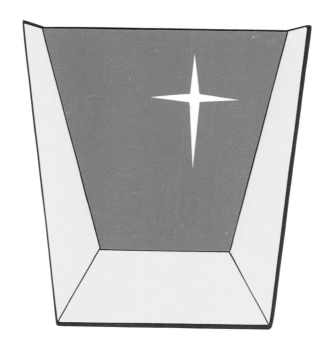

HISPANO-SUIZA *Spain, France*

The Swiss engineer Marc Birkigt had been concerned in making self-propelled vehicles in Spain before the end of the nineteenth century, but by 1901 was making a car in Barcelona called the Castro. Three years later its manufacturers were reorganized as the S.A. Hispano-Suiza and it was renamed accordingly. The name represented the fusion of Spanish capital with Swiss technological know-how, which produced a long line of cars famous in motor sport and also the premier luxury makes of two countries: Spain and France. A Paris factory was set up in 1910, which never built as many cars as the parent, but which, because of the world renown gained by the model it alone made, the H6B of 1919, overshadowed the Barcelona works. The products of the latter were made until 1944, after which commercial vehicles took over, and the last passenger car, a prototype only, emerged from Paris two years later. The emblem shown represents, above the wings (which represent speed), the national colours of Spain (red and yellow), and below, the white cross on a red ground of Switzerland. The circle with radii between the wings represents a turning wheel, while the circle enclosing national colours and wheel symbolized the union between the two countries.

PEGASO *Spain*

Since the death of the Spanish-built Hispano-Suiza in 1942, the Pegaso has been that country's only luxury car—a fitting successor, with its high standards of performance, complexity, and price. A product of Spain's most famous car designer, Wilfredo Ricart, it was made fitfully, in very small numbers, from 1951 to 1964. The manufacturers were the Empress Nacional de Autocamiones (E.N.A.S.A.), who had taken over Hispano-Suiza. E.N.A.S.A. were aircraft as well as truck manufacturers to the government, with well-equipped factories. They dropped the car because it was too expensive and insufficiently refined to sell. The name and emblem was that of Pegasus, the winged horse of Greek mythology that sprang from the trunk of Medusa after Perseus cut off the latter's head. The hero Bellerophon tamed Pegasus with a bridle given to him by Athena, but earned the wrath of the gods by trying to fly up to Heaven. He was thrown by Pegasus and lamed. Afterwards, Pegasus served Zeus. Pegasus was chosen by the manufacturers because he represented the hunter and the warhorse, combining their virtues of speed and strength without the extremes of the temperamental racehorse or of the lumbering draught horse.

SAAB *Sweden*

The initials S.A.A.B., forming the name of one of Sweden's two best-known motor cars, stand for Svenska Aeroplan Aktiebolaget, or Swedish Aeroplane Company, founded in 1937. The emblem, showing the Saab 18, one of the company's first aircraft, was designed in 1941 by Olof Norelius. The first Saab car, based on the D.K.W. from Germany, with its front-wheel drive and two-stroke engine, was introduced in 1950, and soon became famous as a competition car in the hands of Scandinavian rally drivers, thanks to its superior roadholding qualities and strength of construction. A one-model policy was only recently abandoned when a vee-four four-stroke engine was introduced alongside the two-stroke. Currently, the firm makes cars, advanced combat aircraft, missiles and electronic computers.

SCANIA-VABIS *Sweden*

The Vagnfabriksaktiebolaget i Sodertalje (Wagon Factory Company in Sodertalje), VABIS for short, was established in 1891. They concentrated on railway rolling-stock, but in 1897 Gustav Erikson designed them a motor car on the lines of the German Benz. Until 1907 only an occasional car was made, but in that year a new factory was built to concentrate on road vehicles. Most of these were for commercial use. Four years later came amalgamation with the Maskinfabriksaktiebolaget Scania of Malmo, who at first imported Humber bicycles, and from 1901 made cars in small numbers. Like Vabis, they concentrated on commercial vehicles. So did the new Aktiebolaget Scania-Vabis, whose name appears on the emblem illustrated, though passenger cars were offered in a small way until the middle 1920s. The design of the emblem belonged to the Scania A.B. It followed that of the front chain wheel of the Scania bicycle. The crowned eagle's head in the centre comes from the city arms of Malmo. Now the company makes commercials only, though in 1948 it began to import the Volkswagen from Germany.

VOLVO *Sweden*

While in Paris during the 1920s, Assar Gabrielsson, who had worked for the SKF ball-bearing concern, noted the great demands on this industry by the French motor-car industry. His speculations on the possibility of setting up a large-scale passenger-car industry in Sweden, which had never had such a thing (the vehicles of Scania Vabis being made only in penny packets), bore fruit in 1926, when experimental cars were on the road. They were built by the new Aktiebolaget Volvo, on American lines. The name was Latin for 'I roll', and the emblem of the arrowed circle followed that of the conventional map sign for iron. The famous iron and steel industry of Sweden provided the raw material of the new car.

AUBURN *U.S.A.*

The Auburn Automobile Company of Indiana was named after the town in which the factory was situated. Charles, Frank and Morris Eckhart began turning out cars in 1900, and by 1903 were making a primitive two-passenger 'gas buggy' of the sort then popular in America. Bigger machines of all sizes followed, and from 1917, only sixes were offered. A measure of fame came with the introduction of the Beauty Six of 1919, a conventional but extremely good-looking machine. However, the make's great days began when in 1924 E. L. Cord became General Manager. He pioneered the long, low line in American cars, making the Auburn more elegant than ever. The ultimate development of the line was the supercharged speedster of the 1930s, of which the last was made in 1937. The Auburn was then involved in the crash of the Cord Corporation, and disappeared with it.

BUICK *U.S.A.*

David Dunbar Buick ran the firm of Buick & Sherwood of Jackson, Michigan, manufacturers of plumbers' fittings and furnishings, before he turned to cars. His first experimental model was made in 1900. Engines were built, and in 1904 the Buick Motor Company of Flint offered its first production car. Only a handful were made. A year later new finance was introduced by William Crapo Durant, production increased twentyfold, and by 1906 Buick had left. In Durant's hands the company formed the nucleus of the General Motors Company. Among other famous men associated with Buick were C. W. Nash and Walter P. Chrysler, both of whom were general managers of the firm before making their names on their own. The name survives in the Buick Division of the General Motors Corporation.

CADILLAC *U.S.A.*

The Cadillac Motor Car Company of Detroit produced its first cars in 1903. They were designed by Henry M. Leland, who had previously been a general engineer, and had built power units for Ransom E. Olds' Oldsmobiles. Leland, before Ford, was the champion of the principle of the interchangeability of parts, one of the foundations of mass-production, and later pioneered electric self-starting and lighting sets in production cars. The Cadillac name and emblem derive from Antoine de la Mothe Cadillac, founder of Detroit in the seventeenth century. The birds in the first and fourth quarterings are merlettes; heraldic adaptations of the martin forming the original arms of the de la Mothe family. The horizontal bar in each quartering is a fess, or military belt of honour, granted to knights for valiant conduct in the Crusades. The second and third quarterings denote the family's broad acres, and, as in the case of the other quarterings, the colours represent various knightly virtues.

CHEVROLET *U.S.A.*

Louis Chevrolet was a Swiss engineer who was engaged in the bicycle trade in France, then in 1901 went to America as the representative of De Dion-Bouton. He raced Fiats and Christies, and by 1909 he was experimenting with his own small car in Detroit, and also with a six-cylinder design on behalf of William Crapo Durant, who had been employing him as a racing driver, at the wheel of Buick cars. Louis' brother Arthur worked for Durant as his chauffeur. The six that Chevrolet had designed was the first Chevrolet car, and at the end of 1911 the Chevrolet Motor Company was launched. Comparatively few cars were built until 1913, when the works moved to Flint and the first production cars left the line. The low-priced Model 490 of 1915 was the company's first major success. In that year Louis departed, going on to design and build the Frontenac racing car independently, with another brother, Gaston. Later he made the Frontenac cylinder head for Fords. Chevrolet became part of General Motors in 1918. The emblem is said to be derived from a wallpaper design seen by Durant in a hotel bedroom.

CHRYSLER *U.S.A.*

Walter P. Chrysler was a fine engineer, unlike most of the other motor industry tycoons of the 1920s, who were merely clever financiers and organizers. Long before he made a car bearing his own name, he had worked for the American Locomotive Company, for General Motors, and for John North Willys of Willys-Overland. In 1923 Chrysler became independent by taking over the Maxwell Motor Company, but in the same year launched his new Chrysler. This was the first thoroughly modern car in the lower price range to appear in America, with its smooth, efficient engine, front-wheel brakes and balloon tyres. The Chrysler enjoyed immediate and enormous success; so much so that within five years, the Chrysler Corporation was the third largest motor manufacturer in the United States. The seal on the emblem presumably stood for quality.

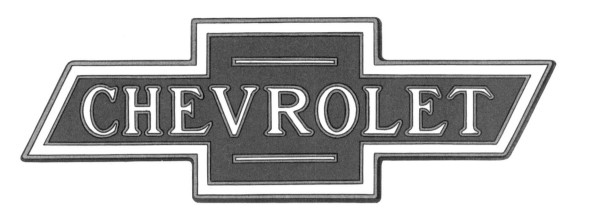

CORD *U.S.A.*

Errett Lobban Cord was an agent for the Moon car who, in 1924, became General Manager of the Auburn Automobile Company. Although the Auburn was already a handsome car, Cord revolutionized its appearance, endowing it with trend-setting long, low lines of great elegance that turned it into a popular fashion leader. In 1926 E. L. Cord gained control of Duesenberg and created the truly fabulous Model J, the biggest, fastest, most elaborate, and most expensive car in America. Feeling the need for a model somewhere in between his two extremes, in 1929 Cord introduced the first car to bear his own name, the L-29 Cord. It, too, was sensational in its way, with its Miller-based front-wheel-drive layout designed by Carl van Ranst. The Cord was too unconventional for the American public, and the L-29 died in 1932. However, the name reappeared in 1935 with the Gordon Buehrig-designed Model 810 Cord, also with front-wheel-drive, and its development the supercharged Model 812. These were the most successful front-wheel-drive cars in America, but even they did not last beyond the dissolution of the Cord Corporation in 1937. The Cord emblem illustrated has much in common with the arms of the M'Cord or Mackorda family of Scotland, and seems to be a modification of it. In the latter, the arrows or pheons were placed in a row on the horizontal band or fess, instead of on the field.

DODGE *U.S.A.*

John and Horace Dodge, bicycle makers, first appeared on the automotive scene making transmissions for the Oldsmobile around the turn of the century. In 1903 the machinist brothers began to provide chassis and engines as well as transmissions for the new Ford car, taking an interest in Henry Ford's firm at the same time. They began to make their own car under their own name in 1914; a well-built, solid, four-cylinder car of completely conventional specification that was the sole Dodge offering until 1927. In its first year, it pioneered the Budd all-steel sedan body. The Dodge four was so successful that it promoted the make to fourth place in the industry within nine years. Both brothers died in 1920, and in 1928 their company was absorbed into the Chrysler Corporation. The Dodge emblem of a globe symbolized world-wide acceptance, but the star had no special significance. The initials D.B. stood, of course, for Dodge Brothers.

DUESENBERG *U.S.A.*

Fred Duesenberg was a bicycle-maker, like so many men who were to pioneer in the motor car field. The first car he designed was the Mason of 1904 onwards. In 1913 he and his brother, August, founded Duesenberg Motors, which built the straight-eight, overhead-camshaft machine that won the French Grand Prix of 1921. This was the first model year of the earliest Duesenberg passenger car, the very advanced, luxurious and expensive Model A, with an in-line eight-cylinder engine, and front-wheel brakes. In both these respects, the Model A was a pioneer among American production cars. The emblem illustrated is that of the Model A. The American eagle that it embodies was first used on Duesenberg products around the time of the First World War, and was very popular on American cars in general at this time, as a patriotic symbol. The great Model J, the A's successor, did not wear a radiator emblem. The fact that it was recognizable as America's biggest, fastest, most complex and most expensive passenger car was considered sufficient identification. This line of Duesenbergs died in 1937 and unsuccessful attempts were made to revive the name with different cars in 1947 and 1966.

FORD *U.S.A.*

Henry Ford ran his first car—which he called his Experimental Quadricycle—in Detroit in 1896. It showed a lot of bicycle characteristics, like so many pioneer cars. Five years later he was in charge of the short-lived Detroit Automobile Company, but launched his own firm, the Ford Motor Company, in 1903. He proceeded to take a sizeable slice of the economy-car market with his Models A, B, C and F, followed by the notably successful Model N of 1906. The most famous Ford of all time was its successor, the Model T of 1908. It was the world's first car to break through to the mass market—only now were conditions favourable enough, the roads beginning to be built and public prejudice overcome. The Model T had the secret of success: it was excellent value, being cheap yet of good quality, simple, and easy to drive. Its parts were standardized and interchangeable, like those of the Cadillac, and they came to be assembled on moving conveyors. So mass-production techniques arrived in the motor-car factory. The type lasted with little change until 1927. Its successor the Model A was overshadowed by the six-cylinder Chevrolet in the same price range, but the Ford V8 of the 1930s did much to restore the company's image.

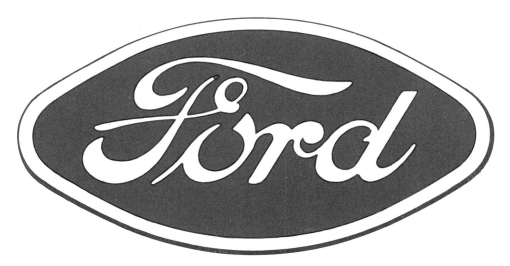

FRANKLIN *U.S.A.*

The Franklin, made by the H. H. Franklin Manufacturing Co. of Syracuse, New York, was the only American car with an air-cooled engine to survive through a normal make life (1902–34). The emblem shown was borne by the 1928 and 1929 'Airman' models on their bonnets, moving to the crankcase in 1930. When air-cooled engines came to predominate in the air, in the later 1920s, the company took full advantage of the publicity won by the pioneer aviators by linking their achievements with the Franklin car. The air-cooled engine, best in the air, was by analogy best on the road. Franklin aero engines followed. The post-Second World War Tucker car was powered by a Franklin helicopter unit.

HUDSON *U.S.A.*

The triangle has been the emblem of the Hudson car since its birth in 1909, but it has no apparent significance. Two are used in the centre of the emblem illustrated. The car is named after J. L. Hudson, the Detroit department store owner who helped to finance it. The ships on the emblem are said to symbolize the adventurous spirit of bold and imaginative engineers. The stylized castle represents the strength and integrity of the manufacturers of the Hudson car, which was made until 1957. In its later years, the name was part of the American Motors Corporation.

HUPMOBILE *U.S.A.*

The Hupp Motor Car Corporation was formed by Louis and Robert Hupp in 1908, who gave their name to the new car. The earliest Hupmobile was one of many attempts being made to offer a cheap four-cylinder runabout in competition with the Model T Ford, but it was not good enough. Its successor, however, provided serious competition in the next highest price class until well into the 1920s. The Hupmobile Eight of 1925 was a landmark in that it was the first attempt to popularize eight-cylinder cars outside the luxury class. The emblem of the Eight is shown here. The company was hard hit by the Depression, and was not strong enough to recover fully. The last cars were made in 1941.

LINCOLN *U.S.A.*

Henry M. Leland, founder of Cadillac, left the company he had launched in 1919, to make another precision-built luxury car. The Lincoln, named after President Abraham Lincoln, lasted under Leland control only until 1922. Henry Ford took it over in that year, and his son Edsel developed it, carrying on Leland's one-model policy. The Ford Lincoln was an improvement in every important way on its predecessor, being endowed with elegant coachwork (which Leland's car emphatically was not), and incorporating mechanical refinements as well. The emblem illustrated dates from this era. A cheap line, called the Lincoln Zephyr, was made from 1936 to 1942. Probably the most famous Lincoln, and one of the most beautiful, was the first-series Continental made in the early 1940s.

LOCOMOBILE *U.S.A.*

Francis E. and Freelan O. Stanley were versatile craftsmen who made violins, home gas generators, photographic dry plates and early X-ray equipment before they turned to motor cars. They made an excellent and successful lightweight steamer in 1897, which was in small-scale production in the same year. Two years later the brothers sold out to A. L. Barber and Brisbane Walker. These gentlemen soon parted, and each made his own version of the Stanley. Walker's was called the Mobile, while Barber's was sold as the Locomobile. In 1902 the Stanley brothers regained control of the steamer, while Locomobile went on to make gasoline runabouts to the designs of A. L. Riker. The Locomobile grew up into a large, luxurious, expensive machine, which gained fame when a Locomobile racing car won the Vanderbilt Trophy in 1908. W. C. Durant took over in 1923, and nine years later the last Locomobile had been built.

MARMON *U.S.A.*

The Nordyke & Marmon Company of Indianapolis were a large firm of millwrights, founded in 1851, as E. & A. H. Nordyke. They were renamed in 1865. Howard C. Marmon had a car built for his own use in 1902. It was successful, and half a dozen more were built in 1903. In the following year the Marmon car was put into production. They were high-quality machines from the beginning, with much aluminium in their construction. A Marmon won the first 500-mile Race held at Indianapolis, in 1911. The last passenger cars were made in 1933, but earlier, Walter C. Marmon and Arthur W. Herrington had broken away to form the Marmon–Herrington Company, specializing in trucks.

MERCER *U.S.A.*

The Mercer was named after Mercer County, New Jersey, where it was made in the town of Trenton. The name became, and remained, famous throughout America with the coming of the Type 35 Raceabout model of 1911, the country's most renowned sport car. The Mercer died in 1925; it appealed to a market that was too small. An attempt to revive it six years later failed when only two cars had been made. The radiator emblem illustrated was used from 1918 until the end. The earliest emblem had included the words 'Trenton N.J.' as well as the make name, while from 1915–17 the model number was substituted for the former.

MERCURY *U.S.A.*

The Mercury, introduced by the Ford Motor Company in 1939, was the brainchild of Edsel Ford. It was designed to be a *de luxe* or 'super'-Ford, coming in a price range between the Ford V8 and the Lincoln Zephyr, the cheap Lincoln. The name chosen for the new model was that of the Roman god, known as Hermes to the Greeks. Shown in the emblem, he was the god of eloquence, and of feats of skill. He was the protector of traders (and of thieves), in his function as presider over the roads. It was in this capacity that he was considered suitable to appear on a car. He was the conductor of departed souls to the Nether World, and the Messenger of the other gods—hence his winged hat (seen in the emblem) and winged sandals.

OLDSMOBILE *U.S.A.*

The Oldsmobile was named after its creator, Ransom E. Olds, who put his immensely popular and famous 'curved-dash' runabout into production in 1901. The firm was a pioneer of some quantity production methods before Ford. General Motors took over the Olds Motor Works at Lansing, Michigan (the words appearing on the emblem) in 1920. The emblem illustrated evolved from a complex crest, retaining only the latter's basic shield shape. The crest had been designed specially for the company, and incorporated a winged spur, symbol of fleetness; three acorns for pioneering quantity production; oak leaves for strength and sturdiness; the lamp of knowledge; and a micrometer and a set-square representing precision. Simplification has something to be said for it.

PACKARD *U.S.A.*

James Ward Packard, an electric lamp manufacturer of Warren, Ohio, designed, but did not build, a car in 1893. He and his brother William Doud Packard bought a Winton car in 1898. Dissatisfied with it, they designed and this time *did* make a car of their own in the following year. They were helped by two former Winton men, G. L. Weiss and W. A. Hatcher. The new machine showed the influence of the Winton and also of the De Dion Bouton from France, a specimen of which Packard had imported. The Ohio Automobile Company was formed for the manufacture of motor cars in 1900, and renamed the Packard Motor Car Company three years later. It moved to Detroit in the same year, 1903. Later, aero and marine engines were also made. The family of the original company's founder, Warren Packard, claimed relationship with the Packers of England. The cross formed of lozenges with a rose (here distorted into a quatrefoil) in each quartering, surmounted by the crest of 'a pelican in her piety'—plucking her breast to feed her young—formed the arms of the Packers of Baddow, Essex. The arms were brought to America by Samuel Packard in the seventeenth century.

PIERCE-ARROW *U.S.A.*

The George N. Pierce Company of Buffalo, New York was founded in 1883, and was known for bird cages and other hardware including bicycles before it turned to motor cars. The first of these was the Pierce Motorette of 1901, a light car powered by a French De Dion engine. From about 1903, the cars came to be called Great Arrows, or Pierce Great Arrows, but from around 1906, the name Pierce-Arrow was adopted. It became applied to one of the most luxurious and expensive cars in America. The Model 66 was also, in its time (until 1917) the biggest production car built in the country. From 1913, headlamps set into the front wings were available, and became a Pierce-Arrow characteristic. Studebaker took control from 1928 until 1933, when the company again became independent. The last Pierce-Arrows were made in 1938. The emblem illustrated was used on the hubcaps from around 1906 to 1928. Only in the latter year was a radiator emblem used.

PLYMOUTH *U.S.A.*

When Chrysler Motors gave up making a four-cylinder Chrysler in 1928, they retained a four-cylinder economy car in their range by substituting the new Plymouth. The Plymouth remained a cheap Chrysler from then on. The name was an evocative one for Americans, being the home town of the Pilgrim Fathers who founded the state of Massachusetts early in the seventeenth century. The ship shown on the emblem represents the *Mayflower*, which carried the Pilgrim Fathers across the Atlantic.

127

PONTIAC *U.S.A.*

In 1907 Edward Murphy of the Pontiac Buggy Company of Pontiac, Indiana, started to build cars under the name of Oakland. The Oakland Motor Car Company was taken over by Durant's General Motors in 1909. In 1926 General Motors introduced a new model into their already very complicated range of cars. The Chevrolet was their cheapest vehicle; above it and just below the Oldsmobile, was the Oakland. Now this six-cylinder car was given a lower-priced, less well-equipped, smaller-engined brother (though one still above the Chevrolet) for which the name Pontiac was revived. In fact, the newcomer turned out to be more popular than the Oakland, so the latter was killed off in 1932. Pontiac was the chief of the Ottawa Indians, leader of the Indian rebellion of 1763–4. This man, remarkable in his ability to unite the tribes, and in his strategic insight, raised the whole western frontier against the British colonies, reducing it to desolation. However, he won none of his expected support from the French, and was defeated. His head is the main feature of the Pontiac emblem. The allusion 'Chief of the Sixes' is obvious.

RAMBLER *U.S.A.*

Thomas R. Jeffery, a well-known bicycle manufacturer, built his first, experimental Rambler car in Chicago in 1896. The Rambler went into production in Kenosha, Wisconsin, five years later, and in the first twelve months sold 1,500 units. This justified Rambler's claim to be the world's second quantity-produced motor car, after the Oldsmobile. An emblem from this period is illustrated. The car was renamed the Jeffery in 1914, and the Jeffery in turn became the Nash when in 1917 Charles W. Nash took over. The Rambler name was revived by Nash in 1950, and from 1958 was used for the cars made by the American Motors Corporation, which had absorbed the Nash-Kelvinator Corporation.

STANLEY *U.S.A.*

The Stanley twins, Francis E. and Freelan O., were manufacturers of a variety of products, including violins, gas generators, photographic plates and X-ray equipment, that had nothing to do with road transportation. However, they produced a very good small steam car in 1897, and put it into production in a small way. In 1899 they sold their rights in the steam car to A. L. Barber and Brisbane Walker for a period of two years, recommencing manufacture in 1902. Production of the Stanley, America's longest-lived steamer, continued until 1924, when the American Steam Automobile Company took the car over. It was made as the Derr for another three years. There was talk late in 1935 of reviving the Stanley, but it came to nothing. The Stanley emblem is elaborate, but it is not known to have any special significance. The central feature is a stylized chariot drawn by four horses abreast, perhaps signifying speed. Flanking it are stems of wheat and hops.

STUDEBAKER *U.S.A.*

The name of Studebaker was famous for wheeled transportation long before the coming of the motor car: first as a maker of wheelbarrows for the miners taking part in the California Gold Rush of 1849. The firm of H. & C. (Henry and Clement) Studebaker was founded at South Bend, Indiana in 1852 as wagon makers and blacksmiths. Their wagons were manufactured in quantity for the United States Army before and during the American Civil War, and at one time Studebaker were the world's largest manufacturer of horse-drawn vehicles. Horse vehicles continued to be made until 1920, but already, in 1902, an electric car had been made, followed a year later by the first Studebaker gasoline car. A merger with the Packard Motor Car Co. came in 1954, and production ceased in 1965. The radiator emblem of the car wheel succeeded the earlier emblem of a wagon wheel.

STUTZ *U.S.A.*

Harry C. Stutz gave his name to one of the most famous sport cars in American automobile history, the Stutz Bearcat speedster of 1914. This car and its less exciting stablemates were made until 1925, though Harry C. Stutz himself had sold out of the business in 1919. He went on to make an inferior vehicle called the H.C.S. on his own account. In 1926 a completely new line of Stutzes made by a new company under Frederick E. Moskovics appeared; machines which, although fast, were also (unlike the old Stutz) modern and comfortable. This was the Vertical Eight or Safety Stutz, which formed the basis for all models made until the end of car production in 1935. The emblem illustrated appeared on the first of the new line of cars, and was used until about 1929.

WILLYS *U.S.A.*

A car called the Overland first appeared on the roads in 1903. Named after the famous overland stage coaches that had helped to open up the West, it was made by the Overland Automobile Division of the Standard Wheel Company. In 1907 the Overland Automobile Company, as it was known by then, faltered in the motor industry depression of that year, but John North Willys, one of its dealers, raised enough money to keep the firm going. It became known as the Willys-Overland Company in 1908, and seven years later, had the second biggest output in the United States after Ford. From 1919 until 1932, the Willys-Knight, with sleeve-valve engine, was built, but the company's most famous vehicle was undoubtedly the wartime Willys Jeep. In 1953, the Henry J. Kaiser interests took over, and the Kaiser Jeep Corporation came into existence. No passenger cars have been made since 1955, production being concentrated on vehicles with the choice of four or two-wheel drive.

WINTON *U.S.A.*

The Winton car was the brainchild of Alexander Winton. Like so many other automobile pioneers, he had made bicycles before he turned to cars, but by 1897 had built a car that ran remarkably well. Winton claimed to be the first motor manufacturer to put a gasoline car of American design and workmanship into production, for he so established his Winton in the spring of 1898. They were simple, reliable machines that were superseded and overshadowed by other new makes, and never regained the predominance they had held at the turn of the century. They continued to be made until 1924, after which Winton concentrated on marine diesel engines. The emblem illustrated is from a Winton Six of 1915. By this time, Wintons were conventional, luxurious and expensive beasts of no special distinction.

MOSKVICH *U.S.S.R.*

The birth of the Moskvich goes back to the period of the Russo-German *entente* prior to the German invasion of Russia in 1941, when a Russian Opel Kadett called the KM10 was made. However, the Moskvich proper was a post-Second World War machine, first produced in 1947, but still based on the pre-war Opel Kadett. As war reparations, the Russians had removed the plant from Germany to Moscow. The letters MZMA on the emblem stand for Moskva Zavod Malolitrazhkaya Avtomobili, or Moscow Small-Engined Car Factory. The red star is, of course, the Soviet emblem.

VOLGA *U.S.S.R.*

The Volga was the updated successor of the Pobieda in the medium-sized family sedan field, though both were made alongside one another in the Molotov Works at Gorki for the first three years of the former's life, 1955–8. The lettering on the emblem reads GAZ, which stands for Gorki Automobile Factory—Gorki Avtomobilnii Zavod. The stag in the emblem formed part of the arms of the city of Nizhni-Novgorod; the old name of Gorki.

ZIL *U.S.S.R.*

The origins of the Zil go back to the Zis. The initials of the latter, which was a copy of the Packard from America and was the Soviet Union's luxury car, stood for Zavod Imieni Stalin, or Stalin Factory, where it was made. After the death and discrediting of Stalin, the car was renamed the Zil—Zavod Imieni Likhatov, Likhatov being the new name of the Moscow factory. The Zil is made only for the upper echelons of government officials, for whom it is a perquisite of office. From being a Packard-like car, the Zil has become more like the General Motors product. The Cyrillic lettering on the emblem reads ZIL.

INDEX